LITTLE PUFFERS

A Guide to Britain's Narrow Gauge Railways 2011-2012

EDITOR
John Robinson

Seventh Edition

RAILWAY LOCATOR MAP

The numbers shown on this map relate to the page numbers for each railway. Pages 5-6 contain an alphabetical listing of the railways featured in this guide. Please note that the markers on this map show the approximate location only.

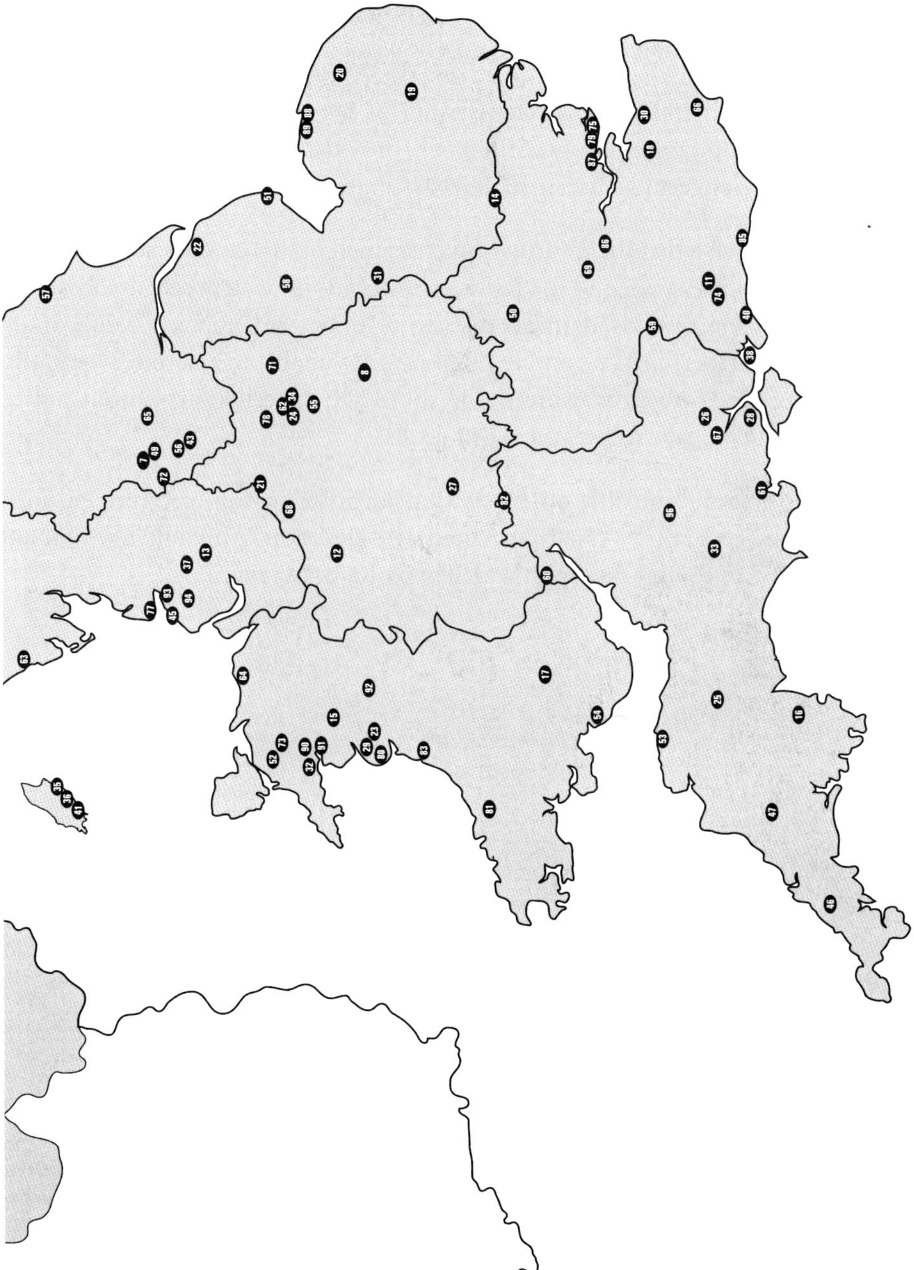

ACKNOWLEDGEMENTS

We were greatly impressed by the friendly and cooperative manner of the staff and helpers of the railways which we selected to appear in this book, and wish to thank them all for the help they have given. In addition we wish to thank Bob Budd (cover design), Michael Robinson (page layouts) and Jonathan James (who provided a number of photographs) for their help.

We are particularly indepted to Peter Bryant for his invaluable assistance. Peter's web site: www.miniaturerailwayworld.co.uk provides a great deal of information about Narrow Gauge and Miniature Railways in the UK.

Although we believe that the information contained in this guide is accurate at the time of going to press, we, and the Railways and Museums itemised, are unable to accept liability for any loss, damage, distress or injury suffered as a result of any inaccuracies. Furthermore, we and the Railways are unable to guarantee operating and opening times which may always be subject to cancellation without notice, particularly during adverse weather conditions.

If you feel we should include other locations or information in future editions, please let us know so that we may give them consideration. We would like to thank you for buying this guide and wish you 'Happy Railway Travelling'!

John Robinson

EDITOR

British Library Cataloguing in Publication Data
A catalogue record for this book is available from the British Library

ISBN-13: 978-1-86223-214-3

Manufactured in the UK by Charlesworth Press

FOREWORD

For the purposes of this publication, we define railways solely by their gauge and include only those with a gauge in excess of 7¼ inches but less than UK Standard gauge. We also publish 'Still Steaming', a separate guide for Standard gauge railways and 'Tiny Trains', a guide for railways with gauges of 7¼ inches and smaller. Both of these guides, as well as further copies of 'Little Puffers' can be ordered UK post free from the Marksman Publications address opposite.

The cover photograph was provided by the Talyllyn Railway, which became the first preserved railway in the world when it was saved from closure in 1951.

CONTENTS

Abbey Light Railway

Address: Bridge Road, Kirkstall, Leeds, LS5 3BW	**Nº of Steam Locos:** None
Telephone Nº: (0113) 267-5087	**Nº of Other Locos:** 12
Year Formed: 1976	**Approx Nº of Visitors P.A.:** 5,000+
Location of Line: Kirkstall Abbey, Leeds	**Gauge:** 2 feet
Length of Line: ¼ mile	**Web site:** www.abbeylightrailway.webs.com

GENERAL INFORMATION

Nearest Mainline Station: Headingley (½ mile)
Nearest Bus Station: Leeds (3 miles)
Car Parking: Available at the Abbey
Coach Parking: Available at the Abbey
Souvenir Shop(s): None
Food & Drinks: Available at the Abbey

SPECIAL INFORMATION

The Abbey Light Railway runs through woodland into the grounds of Kirkstall Abbey.

OPERATING INFORMATION

Opening Times: Sundays and Bank Holidays throughout the year (weather permitting) from 1.00pm to 5.00pm.
Steam Working: Possible with visiting Locos only. Please contact the railway for further information.
Prices: Adult return £2.00 (Single fares £1.00)
Child return £1.00 (Single fares 50p)

Detailed Directions by Car:
From All Parts: From the centre of Leeds, take the A65 (Kirkstall Road) for about 3 miles to the Abbey which is located just to the side of the A65.

Abbey Pumping Station

Address: Abbey Pumping Station Museum, Corporation Road, Leicester, LE4 5PX
Telephone Nº: (0116) 299-5111
Year Formed: 1980s
Location of Line: Leicester
Length of Line: 300 yards

Nº of Steam Locos: 1
Nº of Other Locos: 4
Nº of Members: Approximately 80
Annual Membership Fee: £8.00 Adult, £10.00 Family
Approx Nº of Visitors P.A.: 60,000
Gauge: 2 feet

GENERAL INFORMATION

Nearest Mainline Station: Leicester London Road (3 miles)
Nearest Bus Station: Leicester (1½ miles)
Car Parking: Free parking available on site (Free parking at the Space Centre on Special Event days)
Coach Parking: Use the Space Centre car park
Souvenir Shop(s): Yes
Food & Drinks: Available on special event days only

SPECIAL INFORMATION

The Museum is situated in the Abbey Pumping Station which, from 1891 to 1964 pumped Leicester's sewage to nearby treatment works. The Museum now collects and displays the industrial, technological and scientific heritage of Leicester and contains rare working examples of Woolf compound rotative beam engines which are in steam on selected days.

OPERATING INFORMATION

Opening Times: The Pumping Station is open daily from February to October, 11.00am to 4.30pm. Trains run on the first Saturday of each month from 2nd April and during some special events, 1.00pm to 5.00pm.
Steam Working: Selected special event days only: 2011 dates: 17th April, 25th & 26th June, 11th September and 4th December.
Prices: Adults £3.50 (Special event days only)
Concessions £2.50 (Special events only)
Family £8.00 (Special event days only)

Detailed Directions by Car:
From All Parts: The Museum is situated next to the National Space Centre, about 1 mile North of Leicester city centre near Beaumont Leys and Belgrave. Brown tourist signs with a distinctive rocket logo provide directions to the NSC from the arterial routes around Leicester and the Museum is nearby.

Alford Valley Railway

Address: Alford Station, Main Street, Alford, Aberdeenshire AB33 8HH
Telephone Nº: (07879) 293934
Year Formed: 1979
Location of Line: Alford – Haughton Park
Length of Line: 1 mile
Nº of Steam Locos: None at present
Nº of Other Locos: 3
Approx Nº of Visitors P.A.: 19,500
Gauge: 2 feet
Web site: www.alfordvalleyrailway.org.uk

GENERAL INFORMATION

Nearest Mainline Station: Insch (10 miles)
Nearest Bus Station: Alford (200 yards)
Car Parking: Available on site
Coach Parking: Available on site
Souvenir Shop(s): Yes
Food & Drinks: No

SPECIAL INFORMATION

The Grampian Transport Museum is adjacent to the Railway and the Heritage Centre also has horse-drawn tractors and agricultural machinery.

OPERATING INFORMATION

Opening Times: 2011 dates: Saturdays, Sundays and Bank Holiday Mondays in April, May, June, September and October. Open daily during July and August. Trains usually run from 12.30pm to 4.00pm. Santa Specials operate during the first two weekends in December when higher fares apply.
Steam Working: None at present
Prices: Adult Return £2.50
Child Return £1.50
Family 'Weekly Pass' £15.00
Season Ticket £30.00

Detailed Directions by Car:
From All Parts: Alford is situated 25 miles west of Aberdeen on the Highland tourist route. Take the A944 to reach Alford.

Almond Valley Light Railway

Address: Almond Valley Heritage Centre, Millfield, Livingston EH54 7AR
Telephone Nº: (01506) 414957
Year Formed: 1993
Location of Line: Livingston
Length of Line: 550 yards

Nº of Steam Locos: None
Nº of Other Locos: 2
Approx Nº of Visitors P.A.: 118,000
Gauge: 2 feet 6 inches
Web site: www.almondvalley.co.uk

GENERAL INFORMATION

Nearest Mainline Station: Livingston North (1 mile)
Nearest Bus Station: Livingston (1 mile)
Car Parking: Available on site
Coach Parking: Available
Souvenir Shop(s): Yes
Food & Drinks: Available

SPECIAL INFORMATION

The railway runs through the grounds of the Almond Valley Heritage Centre which hosts a wide range of other attractions including a farm, a historic Mill, nature trails and picnic areas.

OPERATING INFORMATION

Opening Times: The Centre is open daily throughout the year but for 25th & 26th December and 1st & 2nd January. The railway operates at weekends between Easter and the end of September, and daily during some holiday periods, from 11.00am to 4.00pm. Please contact Almond Valley for further details.
Steam Working: None at present.
Prices: Adults £5.00 (Admission to Centre)
Children £3.50 (Admission to Centre)
Family £17.00 (Admission to Centre)
Note: Train rides are an extra £1.00 per person.

Detailed Directions by Car:
From All Parts: Exit the M8 at Junction 3A and take the A779 towards Livingston. Almond Valley Heritage Centre is located near the junction of the A779 and the A705 and is clearly signposted.

Amberley Museum & Heritage Centre

Address: Amberley Museum & Heritage Centre, Amberley, Arundel BN18 9LT
Telephone Nº: (01798) 831370
Year Formed: 1979
Location of Line: Amberley
Length of Line: ¾ mile

Nº of Steam Locos: 3
Nº of Other Locos: 20+
Nº of Members: 300 volunteers
Annual Membership Fee: £22.00
Approx Nº of Visitors P.A.: 60,000
Gauge: 2 feet
Web site: www.amberleymuseum.co.uk

GENERAL INFORMATION

Nearest Mainline Station: Amberley (adjacent)
Nearest Bus Station: –
Car Parking: Free parking available on site
Coach Parking: Free parking available on site
Souvenir Shop(s): Yes
Food & Drinks: Yes

SPECIAL INFORMATION

Amberley Museum covers 36 acres of former chalk pits and comprises over 30 buildings containing hundreds of different exhibits.

OPERATING INFORMATION

Opening Times: 2011 dates: Tuesday to Sunday from 9th April to 30th October and also on Bank Holidays. Trains run from 10.00am to 5.30pm
Steam Working: Please phone for details.
Prices: Adult £9.80
Child £6.00 (free for Under-5's)
Concessions £8.80
Family £29.00 (2 adults + 3 children)

Detailed Directions by Car:
From All Parts: Amberley Museum is situated in West Sussex on the B2139 mid-way between Arundel and Storrington and is adjacent to Amberley Railway Station.

Amerton Railway

Address: Amerton Farm, Stow-by-Chartley, Staffordshire ST18 0LA
Telephone Nº: (01785) 850965
Year Formed: 1991
Location: Amerton Farm
Length of Line: Approximately 1 mile

Nº of Steam Locos: 2
Nº of Other Locos: 7
Nº of Members: 45
Approx Nº of Visitors P.A.: 30,000
Gauge: 2 feet
Web site: www.amertonrailway.co.uk

GENERAL INFORMATION

Nearest Mainline Station: Stafford (8 miles)
Nearest Bus Station: Stafford (8 miles)
Car Parking: Free parking available on site
Coach Parking: Available by arrangement
Souvenir Shop(s): Yes
Food & Drinks: Yes

SPECIAL INFORMATION

The Railway is run by volunteers and the circuit was completed in 2002. The Summer Steam Gala in 2011 will be held on 18th & 19th June.

OPERATING INFORMATION

Opening Times: Weekends from the end of March to the end of October and on Tuesdays, Wednesdays and Thursdays during the School Holidays. Also open for Santa Specials in December. Open from midday to 5.00pm at weekends but only until 4.00pm during midweek dates.
Steam Working: Sundays and Bank Holidays only.
Prices: Adult £2.20
Child £1.50
Concession £1.70

Detailed Directions by Car:
Amerton is located on the A518, 1 mile from the junction with the A51 – Amerton Farm is signposted at the junction. The Railway is located approximately 8 miles from Junction 14 of the M6.

Astley Green Colliery Museum

Address: Higher Green Lane,
Astley Green, Tyldesley M29 7JB
Telephone Nº: (01942) 708969
Year Formed: 1983
Location of Line: Astley Green Colliery
Length of Line: 440 yards

Nº of Steam Locos: None
Nº of Other Locos: 33
Nº of Members: 120
Approx Nº of Visitors P.A.: 6,000
Gauge: 2 feet
Web site: www.agcm.org.uk

GENERAL INFORMATION

Nearest Mainline Station: Salford (3 miles)
Nearest Bus Station: Manchester (5 miles)
Car Parking: Available on site
Coach Parking: Available
Souvenir Shop(s): None
Food & Drinks: None

SPECIAL INFORMATION

Astley Green Colliery Museum houses the largest collection of underground colliery locos in the UK. The 440 yard line is used for freight demonstrations.

OPERATING INFORMATION

Opening Times: Tuesday, Thursday and Sunday throughout the year except for Christmas Day and Boxing Day. Also open at other times by prior arrangement. Open from 1.30pm to 5.00pm.
Steam Working: None
Prices: No admission charge but donations are gratefully accepted.
Note: The museum does not offer passenger rides.

Detailed Directions by Car:
From All Parts: Exit the M6 at Junction 23 and take the A580 towards Manchester. After about 6 miles cross the Bridgewater Canal then take the next right signposted Higher Green. After approximately ¼ mile turn left into the Colliery grounds.

Audley End Steam Railway

Address: Audley End, Saffron Walden, Essex
Telephone Nº: (01799) 541354
Year Formed: 1964
Location of Line: Opposite Audley End House, Saffron Walden
Length of Line: 1½ miles
Nº of Steam Locos: 6
Nº of Other Locos: 3
Approx Nº of Visitors P.A.: 42,000
Gauge: 10¼ inches
Web site: www.audley-end-railway.co.uk

GENERAL INFORMATION

Nearest Mainline Station: Audley End (1 mile)
Nearest Bus Station: Saffron Walden (1 mile)
Car Parking: Available on site
Coach Parking: Available on site
Souvenir Shop(s): Yes
Food & Drinks: Snacks available

SPECIAL INFORMATION

Audley End Steam Railway is Lord Braybrooke's private miniature railway situated just next to Audley End House, an English Heritage site. Private parties can be catered for outside of normal running hours.

OPERATING INFORMATION

Opening Times: 2011 dates: Weekends from 26th March to 30th October and also daily during School Holidays. Also Santa Specials in December. Trains run from 2.00pm (11.00am on Bank Holidays).
Steam Working: Weekends and Bank Holidays.
Prices: Adult Return £3.50
Child Return £2.50
Santa Specials £5.00
Note: Multi-ride tickets are also available.

Detailed Directions by Car:
Exit the M11 at Junction 10 if southbound or Junction 9 if northbound and follow the signs for Audley End House. The railway is situated just across the road from Audley End House.

Bala Lake Railway

Address: Bala Lake Railway,
Llanuwchllyn, Gwynedd, LL23 7DD
Telephone N°: (01678) 540666
Year Formed: 1972
Location of Line: Llanuwchllyn to Bala
Length of Line: 4½ miles

N° of Steam Locos: 5 (all are not in
N° of Other Locos: 3 working order)
Approx N° of Visitors P.A.: 20,000
Gauge: 1 foot 11 five-eighth inches
Web site: www.bala-lake-railway.co.uk

GENERAL INFORMATION

Nearest Mainline Station: Wrexham (40 miles)
Nearest Bus Station: Wrexham (40 miles)
Car Parking: Adequate parking in Llanuwchllyn
Coach Parking: At Llanuwchllyn or in Bala Town Centre
Souvenir Shop(s): Yes
Food & Drinks: Yes – unlicensed!

SPECIAL INFORMATION

Bala Lake Railway is a narrow-gauge railway which follows 4½ miles of the former Ruabon to Barmouth G.W.R. line.

OPERATING INFORMATION

Opening Times: Easter until the end of September closed on Mondays and Fridays (excepting Bank Holidays) in April, May, June and September.
Steam Working: All advertised services are steam hauled. Trains run from 11.15am to 4.00pm.
Prices: Adult Single £6.50; Return £9.50
Child Single £2.50; Return £3.00
Senior Citizen Return £9.00
Family Tickets (Return): £11.50 (1 Adult + 1 Child); £23.00 (2 Adults + 2 Children).
Additional Children pay £2.50 each.
Under 5's and dogs travel free of charge!

Detailed Directions by Car:
From All Parts: The railway is situated off the A494 Bala to Dolgellau road which is accessible from the national motorways via the A5 or A55.

Bickington Steam Railway

Address: Trago Mills Shopping & Leisure Centre, Stover, Devon TQ12 6JB
Telephone Nº: (01626) 821111
Year Formed: 1988
Location of Line: Near the junction of A38 and A382
Length of Line: 1½ miles

Nº of Steam Locos: 4
Nº of Other Locos: 1
Approx Nº of Visitors P.A.: Not known
Gauge: 10¼ inches
Web site: freespace.virgin.net/hanson.mike/Tragorailway.htm

GENERAL INFORMATION

Nearest Mainline Station: Newton Abbott (3½ miles)
Nearest Bus Station: Newton Abbott
Car Parking: Free parking available on site
Coach Parking: Available on site
Souvenir Shop(s): Yes
Food & Drinks: Available adjacent to the Railway

SPECIAL INFORMATION

Bickington Steam Railway is part of the Trago Mills Shopping & Leisure Centre which occupies around 100 acres of rolling South Devon countryside. The site has numerous other attractions including, 'The Finest 00-gauge Model Railway in the UK'!

OPERATING INFORMATION

Opening Times: Monday to Saturday 11.00am to 5.00pm and Sundays 12.00pm to 4.00pm.
Steam Working: Most operating days but please contact the Railway for precise information.
Prices: £4.99 for a Day Ticket which gives 10 rides.

Detailed Directions by Car:
From All Parts: Take the M5 from Exeter to the A38 and head towards Plymouth. Exit at the junction with the A382 and follow the signs for 'Trago Mills'. The railway is situated on this road after about 1 mile.

Brecon Mountain Railway

Address: Pant Station, Dowlais, Merthyr Tydfil CF48 2UP	**Gauge:** 1 foot 11¾ inches
Telephone Nº: (01685) 722988	**Length of Line:** 5 miles (3½ in service)
Year Formed: 1980	**Nº of Steam Locos:** 8
Location of Line: North of Merthyr Tydfil – 1 mile from the A465	**Nº of Other Locos:** 3
	Approx Nº of Visitors P.A.: 75,000
	Web: www.breconmountainrailway.co.uk

GENERAL INFORMATION

Nearest Mainline Station: Merthyr Tydfil (3 miles)
Nearest Bus Station: Merthyr Tydfil (3 miles)
Car Parking: Available at Pant Station
Coach Parking: Available at Pant Station
Souvenir Shop(s): Yes
Food & Drinks: Yes – including licensed restaurant

SPECIAL INFORMATION

It is possible to take a break before the return journey at Pontsticill to have a picnic, take a forest walk or visit the lakeside snackbar and play area.

OPERATING INFORMATION

Opening Times: Weekends and Bank Holidays throughout the year and daily during School holidays. Daily from the start of April to the end of October but closed on some Mondays and Fridays in April, May, September and October. Open almost every day in December for Santa Specials. Trains typically run from 11.00am to 4.00pm and from 12.00pm to 3.00pm during off-peak times.
Steam Working: Most services are steam hauled.
Prices: Adults £10.00
Children £5.00 (Ages 2 and under ride free)
Senior Citizens £9.25
Note: Two children can travel for £4.00 each when accompanying a paying adult.

Detailed Directions by Car:
Exit the M4 at Junction 32 and take the A470 to Merthyr Tydfil. Go onto the A465 and follow the brown tourist signs for the railway.

Bredgar & Wormshill Light Railway

Address: The Warren, Bredgar, near Sittingbourne, Kent ME9 8AT
Telephone Nº: (01622) 884254
Year Formed: 1972
Location of Line: 1 mile south of Bredgar
Length of Line: ¾ mile
Gauge: 2 feet
Nº of Steam Locos: 10
Nº of Other Locos: 2
Approx Nº of Visitors P.A.: 7,000
Web site: www.bwlr.co.uk

GENERAL INFORMATION

Nearest Mainline Station:
Hollingbourne (3 miles) or Sittingbourne (5 miles)
Nearest Bus Station: Sittingbourne
Car Parking: 500 spaces available – free parking
Coach Parking: Free parking available by appointment
Souvenir Shop(s): Yes
Food & Drinks: Yes

SPECIAL INFORMATION

A small but beautiful railway in rural Kent. The railway also has other attractions including a Model Railway, Traction Engines, a working Beam Engine, Vintage cars, a Locomotive Shed, a picnic site and woodland walks.

OPERATING INFORMATION

Opening Times: Open on Easter Sunday then the first Sunday of the month from May to October. Open from 10.30am to 5.00pm
Steam Working: 11.00am to 4.30pm
Prices: Adult £7.50 Child £3.00

Detailed Directions by Car:
Take the M20 and exit at Junction 8 (Leeds Castle exit). Travel 4½ miles due north through Hollingbourne. The Railway is situated a little over 1 mile south of Bredgar village.

BRESSINGHAM STEAM EXPERIENCE

Address: Bressingham Steam Museum, Bressingham, Diss, Norfolk IP22 2AB
Telephone Nº: (01379) 686900
Year Formed: Mid 1950's
Location of Line: Bressingham, Near Diss
Length of Line: 5 miles in total (3 lines)

Nº of Steam Locos: Many Steam locos
Nº of Members: 70 volunteers
Approx Nº of Visitors P.A.: 80,000+
Gauge: Standard, 2 foot, 10¼ inches and 15 inches
Web site: www.bressingham.co.uk

GENERAL INFORMATION

Nearest Mainline Station: Diss (2½ miles)
Nearest Bus Station: Bressingham (1¼ miles)
Car Parking: Free parking for 400 cars available
Coach Parking: Free parking for 30 coaches
Souvenir Shop(s): Yes
Food & Drinks: Yes

SPECIAL INFORMATION

In addition to Steam locomotives, Bressingham has a large selection of steam traction engines, fixed steam engines and also the National Dad's Army Museum, two extensive gardens and a water garden centre.

OPERATING INFORMATION

Opening Times: 2011 dates: Daily from 31st March to 30th October. Open from 10.30am to 5.00pm and until 5.30pm in June, July and August.
Steam Working: Almost every operating day except for most Mondays and Tuesdays in March, April, May, June, July, September and October. Please phone the Museum for further details.
Prices: Adult £10.00 (non-Steam) £12.50 (Steam)
Child £6.50 (non-Steam) £8.50 (Steam)
Family £27.50 (non-Steam) £35.00 (Steam)
Seniors £9.00 (non-Steam) £11.00 (Steam)

Detailed Directions by Car:
From All Parts: Take the A11 to Thetford and then follow the A1066 towards Diss for Bressingham. The Museum is signposted by the brown tourist signs.

Bure Valley Railway

Address: Aylsham Station, Norwich Road, Aylsham, Norfolk NR11 6BW
Telephone Nº: (01263) 733858
Year Formed: 1989
Location of Line: Between Aylsham and Wroxham
Length of Line: 9 miles

Nº of Steam Locos: 5
Nº of Other Locos: 3
Approx Nº of Visitors P.A.: 120,000
Gauge: 15 inches
Web Site: www.bvrw.co.uk
e-mail: info@bvrw.co.uk

GENERAL INFO

Nearest Mainline Station:
Wroxham (adjacent)
Nearest Bus Station:
Aylsham (bus passes station)
Car Parking: Free parking at Aylsham and Wroxham Stations
Coach Parking: As above
Souvenir Shop(s): Yes at both Stations
Food & Drinks: Yes (a Café at Aylsham also opens daily)

SPECIAL INFO

Boat trains connect at Wroxham with a 1½ hour cruise on the Norfolk Broads. Steam Locomotive driving courses are available throughout the year except in July and August. Some carriages are able to carry wheelchairs.

OPERATING INFO

Opening Times: Aylsham Station is open daily. Trains run on various dates in 2011 from 19th February to the end of October. Open during weekends in March and daily from 2nd April to 31st October plus some other dates. Trains run from 10.00am to 5.35pm during high season. Open for Santa Specials on dates in December. Please contact the railway for further details.
Steam Working:
Most trains are steam hauled
Prices: Adult Return £12.00
(Single £8.00)
Child Return £6.50
(Single £5.00)
Family Return £32.00
(2 adult + 2 child)
Party discounts are available for groups of 20 or more if booked in advance.

Detailed Directions by Car:
From Norwich: Aylsham Station is situated midway between Norwich and Cromer on the A140 – follow the signs for Aylsham Town Centre. Wroxham Station is adjacent to the Wroxham British Rail Station – take the A1151 from Norwich; From King's Lynn: Take the A148 and B1354 to reach Aylsham Station.
Satellite Navigation: Use NR11 6BW for Aylsham Station and NR12 8UU for Wroxham Station.

Buxton Miniature Railway

Address: Pavilion Gardens,
St. John's Road, Buxton SK17 6BE
Telephone Nº: (01298) 23114
Year Formed: 1972
Location of Line: Buxton, Derbyshire
Length of Line: 320 yards

Nº of Steam Locos: None
Nº of Other Locos: 1
Approx Nº of Visitors P.A.: Not known
Gauge: 12¼ inches
Web site: www.paviliongardens.co.uk

GENERAL INFORMATION

Nearest Mainline Station: Buxton (350 yards)
Nearest Bus Station: Buxton
Car Parking: Available on site – Pay & Display
Coach Parking: Available
Souvenir Shop(s): Yes
Food & Drinks: Available

SPECIAL INFORMATION

The railway is located in the Buxton Pavilion Gardens, an historic venue of 23 acres situated in the heart of Buxton which was first opened in 1871.

OPERATING INFORMATION

Opening Times: Weekends throughout the year, weather permitting and daily during the school holidays. Open from 9.30am to 5.00pm.
Steam Working: None at present.
Prices: Adults £1.00
Children £1.00 (Under-3s ride for free)

Detailed Directions by Car:
From All Parts: The railway is located in Pavilion Gardens in Buxton which is at the side of the A53 (St. John's Road) and just opposite the junction with the A5004 (Manchester Road).

CLEETHORPES COAST LIGHT RAILWAY

Address: King's Road, Cleethorpes, North East Lincolnshire DN35 0AG
Telephone Nº: (01472) 604657
Year Formed: 1948
Location of Line: Lakeside Park & Marine embankment along Cleethorpes seafront
Length of Line: Almost 2 miles
Nº of Steam Locos: 9
Nº of Other Locos: 4
Nº of Members: 200
Annual Membership Fee: Adult £11.00
Approx Nº of Visitors P.A.: 120,000
Gauge: 15 inches
Web: www.cleethorpescoastlightrailway.co.uk

GENERAL INFORMATION

Nearest Mainline Station: Cleethorpes (1 mile)
Nearest Bus Stop: Meridian Point (opposite)
Car Parking: Boating Lake car park – 500 spaces (fee charged)
Coach Parking: As above
Souvenir Shop(s): Yes
Food & Drinks: Brief Encounters Tearoom on Lakeside Station

SPECIAL INFORMATION

A line extension to Humberston opened in 2008.

OPERATING INFORMATION

Opening Times: 2011 dates: Open daily from 9th April to 1st May, 28th May to 4th September and 10th September to 30th October. Closed in November but open for Santa Specials during December. Also open on weekends, Bank holidays and school holidays at other times. Trains run from 11.00am to 4.20pm in Winter, 6.00pm in Summer.
Steam Working: Most services are steam hauled
Prices: Adult Return £3.90 Child Return £3.50
Family Return £12.00 (2 Adult + 2 Child)
Note: Lower prices apply for shorter journeys.

Detailed Directions by Car:
Take the M180 to the A180 and continue to its' end. Follow signs for Cleethorpes. The Railway is situated along Cleethorpes seafront 1 mile south of the Pier. Look for the brown Railway Engine tourist signs and the main station is adjacent to the Leisure Centre.

The Corris Railway

Address: Station Yard, Corris, Machynlleth, Mid Wales SY20 9SH
Telephone Nº: (01654) 761303
Year Formed: 1966
Location of Line: Corris to Maespoeth, Mid Wales
Length of Line: ¾ mile

Nº of Steam Locos: 1
Nº of Other Locos: 4
Nº of Members: 500
Annual Membership Fee: £15.00 (adult)
Approx Nº of Visitors P.A.: 7,000
Gauge: 2 feet 3 inches
Web site: www.corris.co.uk

GENERAL INFORMATION

Nearest Mainline Station: Machynlleth (5 miles)
Nearest Bus Station: Machynlleth (5 miles)
Car Parking: Available on site and also at the Corris Craft Centre (500 yards)
Coach Parking: Corris Craft Centre (please pre-book if visiting)
Souvenir Shop(s): Yes
Food & Drinks: Yes

SPECIAL INFORMATION

The Corris Railway Society was formed in 1966 and the line itself dates back to 1859. The Railway's new-build 'Tattoo' class steam locomotive was delivered on 17th May 2005.

OPERATING INFORMATION

Opening Times: 2011 dates: Open from Good Friday until 2nd May then every Sunday until the end of September, some Saturdays in May and June, all Saturdays in July and August, Mondays and Tuesdays in August and on all Bank Holiday weekends. The first train leaves Corris Station at 11.00am, last train at 4.00pm
Steam Working: Most trains are steam-hauled.
Prices: Adult Return £5.00
Child Return £2.50
Senior Citizen Return £4.50
Family Return £12.50
(2 adults + 2 children)

Detailed Directions by Car:
From All Parts: Corris is situated off the A487 trunk road, five miles north of Machynlleth and 11 miles south of Dolgellau. Turn off the trunk road at the Braichgoch Hotel and the Station Yard is the 2nd turn on the right as you enter the village, just past the Holy Trinity Church.

DERBYSHIRE DALES NARROW GAUGE RAILWAY

Correspondence: 44 Midland Terrace, Westhouses, Alfreton DE55 5AB
Contact Phone Nº: (01629) 580381
Year Formed: 1998
Location of Line: Rowsley South Station, Peak Rail
Length of Line: 500 yards

Nº of Steam Locos: None
Nº of Other Locos: 7
Approx Nº of Visitors P.A.: Not known
Gauge: 2 feet
Web site: www.peakrail.co.uk

GENERAL INFORMATION

Nearest Mainline Station: Matlock (4 miles)
Nearest Bus Station: Matlock (4 miles)
Car Parking: 200 spaces at Rowsley South Station
Coach Parking: Free parking at Rowsley South
Souvenir Shop(s): Yes
Food & Drinks: Yes

SPECIAL INFORMATION

This narrow gauge line is operated at Peak Rail's Rowsley South Station. The line has now been extended to 500 yards.

OPERATING INFORMATION

Opening Times: Sundays and Bank Holiday weekends from April to early October.
Also open on certain Wednesdays in July and August – please contact the railway for further information.
Steam Working: None at present.
Prices: Adult £1.00
Children 25p

Detailed Directions by Car:
Follow the A6 Bakewell to Matlock road to Rowsley then follow the brown tourist signs for the Peak Rail Station.

Devon Railway Centre

Address: Bickleigh, Tiverton, Devon, EX16 8RG
Telephone Nº: (01884) 855671
Year Formed: 1997
Location of Line: Bickleigh, Devon
Length of Line: ½ mile (2 foot and 7¼ inch gauges); 200 yards (Standard gauge)

Nº of Steam Locos: 3
Nº of Other Locos: 19
Approx Nº of Visitors P.A.: Not recorded
Gauge: 2 feet, 7¼ inches and Standard
Web site: www.devonrailwaycentre.co.uk

GENERAL INFORMATION

Nearest Mainline Station: Exeter
Nearest Bus Station: Tiverton (Route 55)
Car Parking: Available on site
Coach Parking: Available on site
Souvenir Shop(s): Yes
Food & Drinks: Yes

SPECIAL INFORMATION

Devon Railway Centre has passenger carrying lines and also features a large model railway exhibition with 15 working layouts. A delightful Edwardian model village has recently been built to a 1:12 scale and there are indoor and outdoor play areas.

OPERATING INFORMATION

Opening Times: 2011 dates: Daily from 9th April to 2nd May, 25th May to 4th September and 22nd to 30th October. Also open Wednesday to Sunday inclusive from 4th to 22nd May, 7th September to 2nd October and during weekends in October. Closed on Mondays during June. Santa Specials run on 10th, 11th, 17th & 18th December. Open from 10.30am until 5.00pm on all operating days.
Steam Working: Trains may be steam or diesel hauled so please phone for further details.
Prices: Adult £6.90 Child £5.50
Senior Citizen £5.70 Family £21.90
Admission includes unlimited train rides and access to the model village, model railways and museum.

Detailed Directions by Car:
From All Parts: Devon Railway Centre is situated adjacent to the famous Bickleigh Bridge, just off the A396 Exeter to Tiverton road (3 miles from Tiverton and 8 miles from Exeter).

Eastleigh Lakeside Steam Railway

Address: Lakeside Country Park,
Wide Lane, Eastleigh, Hants. SO50 5PE
Telephone Nº: (023) 8061-2020
Year Formed: 1992
Location: Opposite Southampton airport
Length of Line: 1¼ miles

Nº of Steam Locos: 18
Nº of Other Locos: 3
Approx Nº of Visitors P.A.: 50,000
Gauge: 10¼ inches and 7¼ inches
Web site: www.steamtrain.co.uk

GENERAL INFORMATION

Nearest Mainline Station: Southampton Airport (Parkway) (¼ mile)
Nearest Bus Station: Eastleigh (1½ miles)
Car Parking: Free parking available on site
Coach Parking: Free parking available on site
Souvenir Shop(s): Yes
Food & Drinks: Cafe on site when railway is open

SPECIAL INFORMATION

The railway also has a playground and picnic area overlooking the lakes.

OPERATING INFORMATION

Opening Times: Weekends throughout the year and daily from mid-July until mid-September plus all other school holidays. Open 10.00am to 4.30pm (until 4.00pm during the winter months).
Santa Specials run on some dates in December.
Steam Working: As above
Prices: Adult Return £3.00 (First Class £3.50)
Child Return £2.50 (First Class £3.00)
Tickets are available offering 3 return journeys at reduced rates. Annual season tickets are available.
Children under the age of 2 years ride free of charge.
Driver training courses can be booked in advance.

Detailed Directions by Car:
From All Parts: Exit the M27 at Junction 5 and take the A335 to Eastleigh. The Railway is situated ¼ mile past Southampton Airport Station on the left hand side of the A335.

EVESHAM VALE LIGHT RAILWAY

Address: Evesham Country Park, Twyford, Evesham WR11 4TP
Telephone Nº: (01386) 422282
Year Formed: 2002
Location of Line: 1 mile north of Evesham
Length of Line: 1¼ miles
Nº of Steam Locos: 6
Nº of Other Locos: 3
Approx Nº of Visitors P.A.: 50,000
Gauge: 15 inches
Web site: www.evlr.co.uk

GENERAL INFORMATION

Nearest Mainline Station: Evesham (1 mile)
Nearest Bus Station: Evesham (1½ miles)
Car Parking: Available in the Country Park
Coach Parking: Available in the Country Park
Souvenir Shop(s): Yes
Food & Drinks: Restaurant at the Garden Centre

SPECIAL INFORMATION

The railway is situated within the 130 acre Evesham Country Park which has apple orchards and picnic areas overlooking the picturesque Vale of Evesham.

OPERATING INFORMATION

Opening Times: Open at weekends throughout the year and daily during school holidays. Trains run from 10.30am to 5.00pm (until 4.00pm during the winter). Please phone for further details.
Steam Working: Daily when trains are running.
Prices: Adult Return £2.20
Child Return £1.60
Senior Citizen Return £1.90

Detailed Directions by Car:
From the North: Exit the M42 at Junction 3 and take the A435 towards Alcester then the A46 to Evesham; From the South: Exit the M5 at Junction 9 and take the A46 to Evesham; From the West: Exit the M5 at Junction 7 and take the A44 to Evesham; From the East: Take the A44 from Oxford to Evesham. Upon reaching Evesham, follow the Brown tourist signs for Evesham Country Park and the railway.

EXBURY GARDENS RAILWAY

Address: Exbury Gardens, Exbury, Near Southampton SO45 1AZ
Telephone Nº: (02380) 891203
Year Formed: 2001
Location of Line: Exbury
Length of Line: 1½ miles
Nº of Steam Locos: 3
Nº of Other Locos: 1
Approx Nº of Visitors P.A.: 55,000
Gauge: 12¼ inches
Web site: www.exbury.co.uk

Photograph courtesy of Gavin Clinton

GENERAL INFORMATION

Nearest Mainline Station: Brockenhurst (8 miles)
Nearest Bus Station: Hill Top (2½ miles)
The New Forest Open Tour Bus visits the gardens 8 times a day between 25th June and 18th September.
Car Parking: Free parking available on site
Coach Parking: Free parking available on site
Souvenir Shop(s): Yes
Food & Drinks: Available

SPECIAL INFORMATION

The railway is located in the world famous Rothschild azalea and rhododendron gardens at Exbury in the New Forest. A walk-through exhibition in the Engine Shed recalls the building of the steam railway.

OPERATING INFORMATION

Opening Times: 2011 dates: Daily from the 19th March to 6th November. Also open for Santa Specials on 10th, 11th, 17th, 18th, 19th & 20th December. Open from 10.00am to 5.00pm (or dusk if earlier).
Steam Working: Most running days from 11.00am (restricted operation in March and September).
Prices: Adult Return £3.50
Child Return £3.50
Note: The above prices do not include admission to the Gardens which is required to visit the railway. Please check the Exbury web site for further details.

Detailed Directions by Car:
From all directions: Exit the M27 at Junction 2 and take the A326 to Dibden. Follow the brown tourist signs for Exbury Gardens & Steam Railway.

FAIRBOURNE RAILWAY

Address: Beach Road, Fairbourne, Dolgellau, Gwynedd LL38 2EX
Telephone Nº: (01341) 250362
Year Formed: 1916
Location of Line: On A493 between Tywyn & Dolgellau
Length of Line: 2 miles

Nº of Steam Locos: 4
Nº of Other Locos: 2
Nº of Members: 197
Annual Membership Fee: £25.00
Approx Nº of Visitors P.A.: 18,000
Gauge: 12¼ inches
Web Site: www.fairbournerailway.com

GENERAL INFORMATION

Nearest Mainline Station: Fairbourne (adjacent)
Nearest Bus Station: Fairbourne (adjacent)
Car Parking: Available in Mainline station car park
Coach Parking: Pay & Display car park 300 yards
Souvenir Shop(s): Yes
Food & Drinks: Yes – licensed Cafes at Fairbourne and Barmouth Ferry Terminus

SPECIAL INFORMATION

There is a connecting ferry service (foot passengers only) from Barmouth to Barmouth Ferry Terminus.

OPERATING INFORMATION

Opening Times: 2011 dates: Open daily from 2nd April until 18th September (closed on Mondays and Fridays except from mid-July to the end of August). Open at weekends until 23rd October then daily from 24th to 29th October. Santa Specials run on 17th and 18th December at 11.30am and 1.30pm.
Steam Working: 11.00am to 3.30pm for normal service. At peak times 10.40am to 4.20pm.
Prices: Adult Return £8.20
Child Return £4.70
Family £18.95 (2 adults + up to 3 children)
Senior Citizen Return £6.90

Detailed Directions by Car:
From A470: Follow signs for Dolgellau and turn left onto A493 towards Tywyn. The turn-off for Fairbourne is located 8 miles south-west of Dolgellau; From South Wales: Follow signs for Machynlleth, then follow A487 towards Dolgellau. Then take A493 towards Fairbourne.

Faversham Miniature Railway

Address: Brogdale Farm, Brogdale Road, Faversham, Kent ME13 8XZ
Telephone Nº: (01795) 474211
Year Formed: 1984
Location of Line: Faversham, Kent
Length of Line: ½ mile at present
Gauge: 9 inches

Nº of Steam Locos: 2
Nº of Other Locos: 9
Nº of Members: 40
Annual Membership Fee: £10.00 Adult, £25.00 Family
Approx Nº of Visitors P.A.: 3,500
Web: www.favershamminiaturerailway.co.uk

GENERAL INFORMATION

Nearest Mainline Station: Faversham (¾ mile)
Nearest Bus Station: None, but a regular bus service travels to Faversham from Canterbury
Car Parking: Available on site
Coach Parking: Available on site
Souvenir Shop(s): Various shops on site
Food & Drinks: Available

SPECIAL INFORMATION

Faversham Miniature Railway is the only 9 inch gauge railway open to the public in the UK.

OPERATING INFORMATION

Opening Times: Sundays and Bank Holiday weekends from 6th March to November from 11.00am to 4.00pm. Also open for Santa Specials on 11th and 18th December 2011 (bookings required by 1st October).
Steam Working: Special steam days only. Please contact the Railway for further details.
Prices: £1.00 per ride

Detailed Directions by Car:
Exit the M2 at Junction 5 and take the A251 towards Faversham. After about ½ mile turn left onto the A2 then left again after ¼ mile turning into Brogdale Road for the Farm and Railway.

Ferry Meadows Miniature Railway

Address: Ham Lane, Nene Park, Oundle Road, Peterborough PE2 5UU
Telephone Nº: (01933) 398889
Year Formed: 1978
Location of Line: Nene Leisure Park
Length of Line: 700 yards
Nº of Steam Locos: Guest locos only
Nº of Other Locos: 2
Approx Nº of Visitors P.A.: Not known
Gauge: 10¼ inches
Web site: www.ferrymeadowsrailway.co.uk

GENERAL INFORMATION

Nearest Mainline Station: Peterborough (2 miles)
Nearest Bus Station: Peterborough (2 miles)
Car Parking: Available adjacent
Coach Parking: Available adjacent
Souvenir Shop(s): Yes
Food & Drinks: Available

SPECIAL INFORMATION

The railway is situated in the Ferry Meadows area of Nene Park in which watersports and other leisure activities are also available.

OPERATING INFORMATION

Opening Times: 2011 dates: Every weekend from 5th March to 30th October and daily during the school holidays and from 2nd July to 4th September. Trains run from 11.30am to 4.30pm.
Steam Working: Bank Holidays and weekends in August when guest steam locomotives operate.
Prices: Adult Return £2.50
Child Return £1.50

Detailed Directions by Car:
Nene Park is situated on the A605 Oundle Road. Follow the brown tourist signs for Nene Valley Park.

FFESTINIOG RAILWAY

Address: Ffestiniog Railway, Harbour Station, Porthmadog, Gwynedd LL49 9NF
Telephone N°: (01766) 516000
Year Formed: 1832
Location of Line: Porthmadog to Blaenau Ffestiniog
Length of Line: 13½ miles
N° of Steam Locos: 12
N° of Other Locos: 12
N° of Members: 5,000
Annual Membership Fee: £26.00
Approx N° of Visitors P.A.: 140,000
Gauge: 1 foot 11½ inches
Web Site: www.festrail.co.uk

GENERAL INFORMATION

Nearest Mainline Station: Blaenau Ffestiniog (interchange) or Minffordd
Nearest Bus Station: Bus stop next to stations at Porthmadog & Blaenau Ffestiniog
Car Parking: Parking available at Porthmadog, Blaenau Ffestiniog, Minffordd and Tan-y-Bwlch
Coach Parking: Available at Porthmadog and Blaenau Ffestiniog
Souvenir Shop(s): Yes
Food & Drinks: Yes

SPECIAL INFORMATION

The Railway runs through the spectacular scenery of Snowdonia National Park and, from 2011, the line has linked up with the Welsh Highland Railway.

OPERATING INFORMATION

Opening Times: Daily service from late March to early November. A limited service operates in the Winter. Please contact the railway for further details.
Steam Working: Most trains are steam hauled.
Prices: Adult £18.50 (All-day Rover ticket)
One child travels free with each adult, additional children travel for half the fare.
Reductions are available for Senior Citizens and groups of 20 or more.
Cheaper fares are also available for single rides and shorter journeys.

Detailed Directions by Car:
Portmadog is easily accessible from the Midlands – take the M54/A5 to Corwen then the A494 to Bala onto the A4212 to Trawsfynydd and the A470 (becomes the A487 from Maentwrog) to Porthmadog. From Chester take the A55 to Llandudno Junction and the A470 to Blaenau Ffestiniog. Both Stations are well-signposted.

Gartell Light Railway

Address: Common Lane, Yenston, Templecombe, Somerset BA8 0NB
Telephone Nº: (01963) 370752
Year Formed: 1991
Location of Line: South of Templecombe
Length of Line: ¾ mile

Nº of Steam Locos: 2
Nº of Other Locos: 3
Approx Nº of Visitors P.A.: 3,000
Gauge: 2 feet
Web site: www.glr-online.co.uk

GENERAL INFORMATION

Nearest Mainline Station: Templecombe (1¼ miles)
Nearest Bus Station: Wincanton
Car Parking: Free parking adjacent to the station
Coach Parking: Adjacent to the station
Souvenir Shop(s): Yes
Food & Drinks: Meals, snacks and drinks available

SPECIAL INFORMATION

The railway is fully signalled using a variety of semaphore, colour-light and shunting signals, controlled by signalmen in two operational signal boxes. Part of the line runs along the track bed of the old Somerset & Dorset Joint Railway.

OPERATING INFORMATION

Opening Times: 2011 dates: 25th April; 2nd May, 30th May; 26th June; 30th/31st July (Steam Rally); 7th, 14th, 21st, 27th & 28th August; 25th September and 30th October.
Trains depart at frequent intervals between 10.30am and 4.30pm.
Steam Working: Every day the railway operates.
Prices: Adult £7.00
Senior Citizen £5.50
Child £3.50
Note: Tickets permit unlimited travel by any train on the day of purchase. Under-5s travel for free.

Detailed Directions by Car:
From All Parts: The Railway is situated off the A357 just south of Templecombe and on open days is clearly indicated by the usual brown tourist signs.

Golden Valley Light Railway

Address: Butterley Station, Ripley, Derbyshire DE5 3QZ
Telephone Nº: (01773) 747674
Year Formed: 1987
Location of Line: Butterley, near Ripley
Length of Line: Four-fifths of a mile
Web site: www.gvlr.org.uk

Nº of Steam Locos: 2
Nº of Other Locos: 17
Nº of Members: 75
Annual Membership Fee: £16.00
Approx Nº of Visitors P.A.: 10,000
Gauge: 2 feet

GENERAL INFORMATION

Nearest Mainline Station: Alfreton (6 miles)
Nearest Bus Station: Bus stop outside the Station
Car Parking: Free parking at site – ample space
Coach Parking: Free parking at site
Souvenir Shop(s): Yes – at Butterley and Swanwick
Food & Drinks: Yes – both sites

SPECIAL INFORMATION

The Golden Valley Light Railway is part of the Midland Railway – Butterley and runs from the museum site through the country park to Newlands Inn Station close to the Cromford Canal and the pub of the same name.

OPERATING INFORMATION

Opening Times: 2011 dates: Weekends and Bank Holidays from April to October and daily from 22nd April to 2nd May, 1st to 5th June and 23rd July to 4th September. Trains run from 11.45am to 4.15pm.
Steam Working: One weekend per month – please contact the railway for further details.
Prices: Adult £2.00
Children £1.00

Detailed Directions by Car:
From All Parts: From the M1 exit at Junction 28 and take the A38 towards Derby. The Centre is signposted at the junction with the B6179.

Great Laxey Mine Railway

Address: Laxey Valley Gardens, Laxey, Isle of Man
Telephone Nº: (01624) 861706 (Secretary)
Year Formed: 2004
Location of Line: Laxey Valley Gardens
Length of Line: 550 yards

Nº of Steam Locos: 2
Nº of Other Locos: 1
Nº of Members: Approximately 300
Annual Membership Fee: £10.00
Approx Nº of Visitors P.A.: 7,000
Gauge: 19 inches
Web site: www.laxeyminerailway.im

GENERAL INFORMATION

Nearest Mainline Station: Laxey, Manx Electric Railway
Nearest Bus Station: Laxey
Car Parking: Available nearby
Coach Parking: Available nearby
Souvenir Shop(s): Yes
Food & Drinks: There are a number of Cafes nearby

SPECIAL INFORMATION

The Great Laxey Mine Railway is the recently restored surface section of the former mine tramway, the first section of which was opened in 1823. Originally worked by ponies, these were replaced by two steam locomotives in 1877. These engines were scrapped in 1935 but the restored line now uses two working replicas. A few minutes walk from the terminus of the railway is the Lady Isabella water wheel, the largest in the world. The railway itself is operated entirely by volunteers.

OPERATING INFORMATION

Opening Times: Every Saturday and Bank Holiday from Good Friday until the end of September. Open for the Thursday in T.T. week (first week in June), Fathers Day in June, for a Childrens Fun Day in August and a Halloween special weekend in October. Trains run from 11.00am to 4.30pm.
Steam Working: All trains are steam-hauled
Prices: Adult Return £1.50
Child Return £1.00

Detailed Directions by Car:
Laxey is situated approximately 8 miles to the north east of Douglas on the A2 coast road.

Groudle Glen Railway

Address: Groudle Glen, Onchan, Isle of Man
Telephone Nº: (01624) 670453 (weekends)
Year Formed: 1982 **Re-Opened:** 1986
Location of Line: Groudle Glen
Length of Line: ¾ mile
Gauge: 2 feet

Nº of Steam Locos: 2
Nº of Other Locos: 3
Nº of Members: 600
Annual Membership Fee: £15.00
Approx Nº of Visitors P.A.: 10,000
Correspondence: 29 Hawarden Avenue, Douglas, Isle of Man IM1 4BP
Web site: www.ggr.org.uk

GENERAL INFORMATION

Nearest Mainline Station: Manx Electric Railway
Nearest Bus Station: Douglas Bus Station
Car Parking: At the entrance to the Glen
Coach Parking: At the entrance to the Glen
Souvenir Shop(s): Yes
Food & Drinks: Coffee and Tea available

SPECIAL INFORMATION

The Railway runs through a picturesque glen to a coastal headland where there are the remains of a Victorian Zoo. The Railway was built in 1896 and closed in 1962.

OPERATING INFORMATION

Opening Times: 2011 dates: Easter Sunday and Monday then Sundays from 8th May to 25th September 11.00am to 4.30pm. Also Wednesday evenings from 22nd June to 24th August – 7.00pm to 9.00pm. Santa trains run on 11th, 17th and 18th December and on Boxing Day.
Steam Working: Contact the Railway for details.
Prices: Adult Return £4.00
Child Return £2.00
Santa train fares £6.00

Detailed Directions by Car:
The Railway is situated on the coast road to the north of Douglas.

HAIGH RAILWAY

Address: Haigh Country Park, Copperas Lane, Haigh, Wigan WN2 1PE
Telephone Nº: (01924) 832895
Year Formed: 1986
Location of Line: Haigh Country Park
Length of Line: 1½ miles
Nº of Steam Locos: None
Nº of Other Locos: 2
Approx Nº of Visitors P.A.: 300,000 (visitors to Haigh Park)
Gauge: 15 inches
Web site: www.wlct.org/leisure/Haigh/haighhome.htm

GENERAL INFORMATION

Nearest Mainline Station: Wigan (3 miles)
Nearest Bus Station: Wigan (3 miles)
Car Parking: Available on site
Coach Parking: Available
Souvenir Shop(s): Yes
Food & Drinks: Available

SPECIAL INFORMATION

The railway is located in Haigh Country Park, 250 acres of grounds surrounding Haigh Hall with magnificent views across the Douglas Valley to the Welsh Hills.

OPERATING INFORMATION

Opening Times: Weekends from Easter to late September. Also open on Bank Holidays and during the School Holidays. Trains run from 12.00pm to 3.30pm.
Steam Working: None at present.
Prices: Adults £1.00
Children £1.00

Detailed Directions by Car:
From All Parts: Exit the M6 at Junction 27 and take the A49 through Standish to Red Rock before following the brown tourist signs for Haigh Country Park.

Hayling Seaside Railway

Address: Beachlands, Sea Front Road, Hayling Island, Hampshire PO11 0AG
Telephone Nº: (02392) 372427
Year Formed: 2001
Location: Beachlands to Eastoke Corner
Length of Line: 1 mile
Web site: www.haylingseasiderailway.co.uk
Nº of Steam Locos: Visiting locos only
Nº of Other Locos: 4
Nº of Members: Approximately 100
Annual Membership Fee: £10.00
Approx Nº of Visitors P.A.: 25,000
Gauge: 2 feet

GENERAL INFORMATION

Nearest Mainline Station: Havant
Nearest Bus Station: Beachlands
Car Parking: Spaces are available at both Beachlands and Eastoke Corner.
Coach Parking: Beachlands and Eastoke Corner
Souvenir Shop(s): Yes
Food & Drinks: Available

SPECIAL INFORMATION

The Railway runs along Hayling Island beach front where there are fantastic views across the Solent to the Isle of Wight.

OPERATING INFORMATION

Opening Times: Every Saturday, Sunday and Wednesday throughout the year and daily during the School holidays. Various specials run at different times of the year – please check the web site or phone the Railway for further details. The first train normally departs at 11.00am from Beachlands.
Steam Working: Visiting locos only. Please contact the railway for further information.
Prices: Adult Return £3.50
Child/Senior Citizen Return £2.00
Family Return £7.00 (2 Adult + 2 Child)
Dogs travel free of charge!

Detailed Directions by Car:
Exit the A27 at Havant Roundabout and proceed to Hayling Island and Beachlands Station following the road signs. Parking is available south of the Carousel Amusement Park. Beachlands Station is within the car park.

Heatherslaw Light Railway

Address: Ford Forge, Heatherslaw, Cornhill-on-Tweed TD12 4TJ
Telephone Nº: (01890) 820244
Year Formed: 1989
Location of Line: Ford & Etal Estates between Wooler & Berwick
Length of Line: Almost 2½ miles

Nº of Steam Locos: 2
Nº of Other Locos: 1
Approx Nº of Visitors P.A.: 30,000
Gauge: 15 inches
Web site: www.ford-and-etal.co.uk or www.heatherslawlightrailway.co.uk

GENERAL INFORMATION

Nearest Mainline Station: Berwick-upon-Tweed (10 miles)
Nearest Bus Station: Berwick-upon-Tweed (10 mls)
Car Parking: Available on site
Coach Parking: Available on site
Souvenir Shop(s): Yes
Food & Drinks: Available

SPECIAL INFORMATION

The Railway follows the River Till from Heatherslaw to Etal Village. All coaching stock is built on site and a new Steam loco arrived early in 2010.

OPERATING INFORMATION

Opening Times: 2011 dates: Daily from 1st April to 30th October. Trains run hourly between 11.00am and 3.00pm
Steam Working: Daily except when maintenance is is being carried out on the engine.
Prices: Adult Return £6.50
Child Return £4.00 (Under 5's: £2.00)
Senior Citizen Return £5.50

Detailed Directions by Car:
From the North: Take the A697 from Coldstream and the railway is about 5 miles along.
From the South: Take the A697 from Wooler and Millfield.

HOTHAM PARK MINIATURE RAILWAY

Address: Hotham Park, Bognor Regis, PO21 1HR
Telephone Nº: 07880 744597
Year Formed: 2007
Location of Line: Bognor Regis
Length of Line: 900 yards

Nº of Steam Locos: None
Nº of Other Locos: 1
Approx Nº of Visitors P.A.: 20,000
Gauge: 12¼ inches
Web site: www.hothamparkrailway.co.uk

GENERAL INFORMATION

Nearest Mainline Station: Bognor Regis (¼ mile)
Nearest Bus Station: Bognor Regis (½ mile)
Car Parking: Available on site
Coach Parking: Available
Souvenir Shop(s): Available on site
Food & Drinks: None

SPECIAL INFORMATION

The railway is located in Hotham Park, a recently restored 18th Century Park situated in the heart of Bognor Regis.

OPERATING INFORMATION

Opening Times: Weekends throughout the year and daily during School Holidays, weather permitting. Trains run from 11.00am to 4.00pm.
Steam Working: None at present.
Prices: Adults £2.50
Children £2.00
Supersaver card £13.00 for 8 rides

Detailed Directions by Car:
From All Parts: Hotham Park is situated by the side of the A259 across the top end of Bognor Regis High Street and opposite Butlins.

Isle of Man Steam Railway

Address: Isle of Man Railways, Banks Circus, Douglas, Isle of Man IM1 5PT
Telephone N°: (01624) 663366
Year Formed: 1873
Location of Line: Douglas to Port Erin
Length of Line: 15½ miles
N° of Steam Locos: 7
N° of Other Locos: 2
Approx N° of Visitors P.A.: 140,000
Gauge: 3 feet
Web site: www.iombusandrail.info

GENERAL INFORMATION

Nearest Mainline Station: Not applicable
Car Parking: Limited parking at all stations
Coach Parking: Available at Douglas & Port Erin
Souvenir Shop(s): Souvenirs are available from all manned stations and from the shop at Port Erin Railway Museum
Food & Drinks: Yes – Douglas & Port Erin stations

SPECIAL INFORMATION

The Isle of Man Steam Railway is operated by the Isle of Man Government. A number of special events are held at the railway throughout the year.

OPERATING INFORMATION

Opening Times: 2011 Dates: Daily from 9th April to 11th September (closed some Mondays in May). Also open during other dates in March, April, September, October and November. Please contact the railway or check the web site for further details.
Steam Working: All scheduled services
Prices: Prices vary with 1, 3, 5 & 7 day Explorer tickets also available which include travel on buses, the Snaefell and Manx Electric Railways and Douglas Corporation Horse Trams. Railcards offering a 50% discount are also available.

Detailed Directions:
By Sea from Heysham (Lancashire) or Liverpool to reach Isle of Man. By Air from Belfast, Dublin, Glasgow, Liverpool, Manchester, Newcastle, Bristol and London. Douglas Station is ½ mile inland from the Sea terminal at the end of North Quay.

KERR'S MINIATURE RAILWAY

Address: West Links Park, Arbroath, Tayside, Scotland
Telephone Nº: (01241) 874074 or 879249
Year Formed: 1935
Location: Seafront, West Links Park
Length of Line: 400 yards

Nº of Steam Locos: 2
Nº of Other Locos: 4
Approx Nº of Visitors P.A.: 10,000
Gauge: 10¼ inches
Website: www.kerrsminiaturerailway.co.uk
E-mail: info@kerrsminiaturerailway.co.uk

GENERAL INFORMATION

Nearest Mainline Station: Arbroath (1½ miles)
Nearest Bus Station: Arbroath (1½ miles)
Car Parking: Available 600 yards from railway
Coach Parking: Available 600 yards from railway
Souvenir Shop(s): Gifts available
Food & Drinks: Cafe stall in West Links Park

SPECIAL INFORMATION

The Railway is Scotland's oldest passenger-carrying miniature railway. It is a family-run enterprise not run for profit which is staffed by volunteers. The track itself runs alongside the Dundee to Aberdeen mainline.

OPERATING INFORMATION

Opening Times: Easter Holidays then weekends from mid-April and in May, June and September. Daily during July and the first half of August then weekends only for the second half of August. Opening times are 11.00am to 4.00pm.
Steam Working: No set pattern but Steam is more likely to be running on Sundays than other dates.
Prices: Adults £1.50
Children £1.00

Detailed Directions by Car:
From All Parts: West Links Park is a seaside location which runs parallel to the A92 Coastal Tourist Route in Arbroath. Turn off the A92 at the West Links Park/KMR sign. The railway is then 600 yards due West along the seafront.

Kirklees Light Railway

Address: Park Mill Way, Clayton West, near Huddersfield, W. Yorks. HD8 9XJ
Telephone Nº: (01484) 865727
Year Formed: 1991
Location of Line: Clayton West to Shelley
Length of Line: 4 miles
Nº of Steam Locos: 4
Nº of Other Locos: 2
Approx Nº of Visitors P.A.: 48,000
Gauge: 15 inches
Web site: www.kirkleeslightrailway.com

GENERAL INFORMATION

Nearest Mainline Station: Denby Dale (4 miles)
Nearest Bus Station: Bus stop outside gates. Take the 435 from Wakefield or the 80 and 81 from Huddersfield/Barnsley.
Car Parking: Ample free parking at site
Coach Parking: Ample free parking at site
Souvenir Shop(s): Yes
Food & Drinks: Yes

SPECIAL INFORMATION

The Railway now has both indoor and outdoor play areas for children and the new Shelley Station Tearooms are now open throughout the year.

OPERATING INFORMATION

Opening Times: 2011 dates: Open every weekend throughout the year and most school holidays during the Winter. Open daily from 28th May to 4th September.
Steam Working: All trains are steam-hauled. Trains run every 40 minutes from 11.00am to 3.40pm
Prices: Adults £7.00
Children (3-15 years) £5.00
Children (under 3 years) Free of charge
Concessions £6.00
Family Ticket £22.00
Note: Prices at Special events may vary.

Detailed Directions by Car:
The Railway is located on the A636 Wakefield to Denby Dale road. Turn off the M1 at Junction 39 and follow the A636 signposted for Denby Dale. Continue for approximately 4 miles then the railway is on the left after passing under the railway bridge and is situated at the top of the Industrial Estate, just before the village of Scissett.

LAKESHORE RAILROAD

Address: South Marine Park,
South Shields NE33 2LD
Telephone N°: (0191) 454-7761
Year Formed: 1972
Location of Line:
Length of Line: 570 yards

N° of Steam Locos: 2
N° of Other Locos: 1
Approx N° of Visitors P.A.: 65,000
Gauge: 9½ inches
Web site: None

GENERAL INFORMATION

Nearest Mainline Station: South Shields (¾ mile)
Nearest Bus Station: Newcastle (11 miles)
Car Parking: Available on the seafront
Coach Parking: Available nearby
Souvenir Shop(s): None
Food & Drinks: Available nearby

SPECIAL INFORMATION

The Lakeshore Railroad runs two American-designed locomotives – hence the name!

OPERATING INFORMATION

Opening Times: Weekends throughout the year and daily from mid-May to mid-September and during other School Holidays except for Christmas. Trains run from 11.00am to 5.00pm.
Steam Working: Daily, subject to availability
Prices: Adults £1.20
Children £1.20 (Free for Under-3s)

Detailed Directions by Car:
From All Parts: Take the A194 into South Shields. The railway is located by the Seafront in South Marine Park and can be found by following the brown tourist signs marked for the 'Seafront'.

LAKESIDE MINIATURE RAILWAY

Address: Esplanade, Southport PR8 1SQ
Telephone Nº: (01772) 745511
Year Formed: 1911
Location of Line: From the Pier to the Funfair along Southport seafront
Length of Line: 800 yards

Nº of Steam Locos: None
Nº of Other Locos: 5
Approx Nº of Visitors P.A.: 40,000
Gauge: 15 inches
Website: www.lakesideminiaturerailway.co.uk

GENERAL INFORMATION

Nearest Mainline Station: Southport (½ mile)
Nearest Bus Station: Southport (½ mile)
Car Parking: Available nearby
Coach Parking: Available nearby
Souvenir Shop(s): Yes
Food & Drinks: Available

SPECIAL INFORMATION

The railway has operated continuously including during times of war since 25th May 1911.

OPERATING INFORMATION

Opening Times: Daily from Easter until the end of October, weather permitting. Trains run from 11.00am to 5.00pm.
Steam Working: None
Prices: Adult Single £2.00 Return £2.50
Child Single £2.00 Return £2.50
(Under-7s pay 50p less per ride)

Detailed Directions by Car:
From All Parts: Take the A565 or A570 to Southport then follow the brown tourist signs for Pleasureland and Lakeside.

Lappa Valley Steam Railway

Address: St. Newlyn East, Newquay, Cornwall TR8 5LX
Telephone Nº: (01872) 510317
Year Formed: 1974
Location of Line: Benny Halt to East Wheal Rose, near St. Newlyn East
Length of Line: 1 mile
Nº of Steam Locos: 2
Nº of Other Locos: 2
Approx Nº of Visitors P.A.: 50,000
Gauge: 15 inches
Web site: www.lappavalley.co.uk

GENERAL INFORMATION

Nearest Mainline Station: Newquay (5 miles)
Nearest Bus Station: Newquay (5 miles)
Car Parking: Free parking at Benny Halt
Coach Parking: Free parking at Benny Halt
Souvenir Shop(s): Yes
Food & Drinks: Yes

SPECIAL INFORMATION

The railway runs on part of the former Newquay to Chacewater branch line. Site also has a Grade II listed mine building, boating, play areas for children and 2 other miniature train rides.

OPERATING INFORMATION

Opening Times: 2011 dates: Daily from 2nd April to 30th October.
Steam Working: 10.30am to 4.30pm or later on operating days
Prices: Adult £10.95 (Off-peak £8.25)
Child £8.75 (Off-peak £6.00)
Family £33.00 (Off-peak £24.00)
(2 adults + 2 children)
Senior Citizen £9.00
(Off-peak £6.35)

Detailed Directions by Car:
The railway is signposted from the A30 at the Summercourt-Mitchell bypass, from the A3075 south of Newquay and the A3058 east of Newquay.

Launceston Steam Railway

Address: The Old Gasworks, St. Thomas Road, Launceston, Cornwall PL15 8DA
Telephone Nº: (01566) 775665
Year Formed: Opened in 1983
Location of Line: Launceston to Newmills
Length of Line: 2½ miles

Nº of Steam Locos: 4 (3 in steam)
Nº of Other Locos: 4
Gauge: 1 foot 11 ⅝ inches
Web site: www.launcestonsr.co.uk

GENERAL INFORMATION

Nearest Mainline Station: Liskeard (15 miles)
Nearest Bus Station: Launceston (½ mile)
Car Parking: At Station, Newport Industrial Estate, Launceston
Coach Parking: As above
Souvenir Shop(s): Yes – also with a bookshop
Food & Drinks: Yes – Cafe, snacks & drinks

OPERATING INFORMATION

Opening Times: 2011 dates: Daily during Easter Week, Whitsun week and during October half-term. Sundays, Mondays and Tuesdays in June. Daily from 3rd July until the 23rd September but closed on Saturdays.
Steam Working: Hourly from 11.00am to 4.00pm.
Prices: Adult £8.75
Child £5.75
Family £25.00 (2 adults + 4 children)
Senior Citizen £7.50
Group rates are available upon application.

Detailed Directions by Car:
From the East/West: Drive to Launceston via the A30 and look for the brown Steam Engine Tourist signs. Use the L.S.R. car park at the Newport Industrial Estate; From Bude/Holsworthy: Take the A388 to Launceston and follow signs for the town centre. After the river bridge turn left at the traffic lights into Newport Industrial Estate and use the L.S.R. car park.

Leadhills & Wanlockhead Railway

Address: The Station, Leadhills, Lanarkshire ML12 6XP
Telephone Nº: None
Year Formed: 1983
Location of Line: Leadhills, Lanarkshire
Length of Line: ¾ mile (at present)

Nº of Steam Locos: None at present
Nº of Other Locos: 6
Nº of Members: Approximately 100
Annual Membership Fee: Adult £10.00
Approx Nº of Visitors P.A.: 3,500
Gauge: 2 feet
Web site: www.leadhillsrailway.co.uk

GENERAL INFORMATION

Nearest Mainline Station: Sanquhar
Nearest Bus Station: Lanark and Sanquhar
Car Parking: Available on site
Coach Parking: Available on site
Souvenir Shop(s): Yes
Food & Drinks: Yes

SPECIAL INFORMATION

Leadhills & Wanlockhead Railway is the highest adhesion railway in the UK with the summit 1,498 feet above sea level.

OPERATING INFORMATION

Opening Times: Weekends and Bank Holidays from Easter until the end of September. Trains run from 11.20am to 4.20pm on operating days.
Steam Working: None at present
Prices: Adult Day Ticket £3.50
Child Day Ticket £1.50
Family Day Ticket £8.00
(2 adults and up to 6 children)

Detailed Directions by Car:
From the South: Exit the M74 at Junction 14 and follow the A702 to Elvanfoot. Turn right onto the B7040 and follow to Leadhills. Turn left at the T-junction and Station Road is a short distance on the left; From the North: Exit the M74 at Junction 13 for Abington and follow signs for Leadhills along the B797. Station Road is on the left shortly after entering Leadhills.

LEEDS INDUSTRIAL MUSEUM

Address: Canal Road, Armley, Leeds, LS12 2QF
Telephone Nº: (0113) 263-7861
Year Formed: 1985
Location of Line: Armley Mills, Leeds
Length of Line: ¼ mile

Nº of Steam Locos: 8 (One in steam)
Nº of Other Locos: 28 (Two operational)
Approx Nº of Visitors P.A.: 25,000
Gauges: 2 feet and 18 inches
Web site: www.leeds.gov.uk/ArmleyMills

GENERAL INFORMATION

Nearest Mainline Station: Leeds City (2 miles)
Nearest Bus Station: Leeds (2 miles)
Car Parking: Available on site
Coach Parking: Available
Souvenir Shop(s): Yes
Food & Drinks: Tea and coffee only

SPECIAL INFORMATION

A number of Leeds-built locomotives are on display at the museum in addition to a variety of static engines and machinery.

OPERATING INFORMATION

Opening Times: Closed on Mondays but otherwise, daily throughout the year. Open on Bank Holiday Mondays, however. Open from 10.00am to 5.00pm (but from 1.00pm to 5.00pm on Sundays).
Steam Working: Bank Holidays and Tuesdays during the school holidays.
Prices: Adults £3.10
Children £1.10
Concessions £1.60
Family Ticket £6.00
Note: The line is used for demonstrations only – unfortunately, rides are not available.

Detailed Directions by Car:
From All Parts: The Museum is located next to the Cardigan Field Leisure Complex which is just to the South of the A65 Kirkstall Road.

Leighton Buzzard Railway

Address: Pages Park Station, Billington Road, Leighton Buzzard, Beds. LU7 4TN
Telephone Nº: (01525) 373888
Year Formed: 1967
Location of Line: Leighton Buzzard
Length of Line: 3 miles

Nº of Steam Locos: 13
Nº of Other Locos: 55
Nº of Members: 400
Annual Membership Fee: £21.00
Approx Nº of Visitors P.A.: 20,000
Gauge: 2 feet
Web site: www.buzzrail.co.uk

GENERAL INFORMATION

Nearest Mainline Station: Leighton Buzzard (2 miles)
Nearest Bus Station: Leighton Buzzard (¾ mile)
Car Parking: Free parking adjacent
Coach Parking: Free parking adjacent
Souvenir Shop(s): Yes **Food & Drinks:** Yes

SPECIAL INFORMATION

The railway was constructed in 1919 to carry sand from local quarries using surplus materials from World War I battlefield supply lines. Now a working museum, it transports passengers and is operated by volunteers.

OPERATING INFORMATION

Opening Times: 2011 dates: Sundays from 13th March to 30th October plus Bank Holiday weekends. Also open on some Saturdays and weekdays. Trains run from mid-morning to late afternoon and Santa Specials run on some dates in December. Please contact the railway or visit their web site for further information.
Steam Working: Most operating days.
Prices: Adult £8.00
Child £4.00
Senior Citizens £6.00
Family Ticket £22.00 (2 Adult + 2 Child)
Family Ticket £18.00 (2 Adult + 1 Child)

Detailed Directions by Car:
Travel to Leighton Buzzard then follow the brown tourist signs showing a steam train. Pages Park Station is ¾ mile to the south of the Town Centre. From the A505/A4146 bypass, turn towards Leighton Buzzard at the roundabout following the 'Narrow Gauge Railway' brown tourist signs.

LINCOLNSHIRE COAST LIGHT RAILWAY

Address: Skegness Water Leisure Park, Walls Lane, Skegness PE25 1JF
Telephone Nº: (01754) 897400
Year Formed: 1960 (re-opened in 2009)
Location of Line: Skegness
Length of Line: ¾ miles

Nº of Steam Locos: 1 awaiting restoration
Nº of Other Locos: 4
Nº of Members: Approximately 50
Approx Nº of Visitors P.A.: 5,000
Gauge: 2 feet
Web site: www.lincolnshire-coast-light-railway.co.uk

GENERAL INFORMATION

Nearest Mainline Station: Skegness (3 miles)
Nearest Bus Station: Skegness (3 miles)
Car Parking: Free parking available on site
Coach Parking: Free parking available on site
Souvenir Shop(s): None
Food & Drinks: Available

SPECIAL INFORMATION

The railway was originally located some distance up the coast at the Cleethorpes/Humberston 'Fitties' before closure during the 1980s.

OPERATING INFORMATION

Opening Times: 2011 dates: 1st, 29th & 30th May; 17th, 24th & 31st July; 7th, 14th, 21st, 28th & 29th August and a Gala weekend on 3rd & 4th September.
Steam Working: Please contact the railway for further details.
Prices: Adults £1.00
Children £1.00

Detailed Directions by Car:
From All Parts: Take the A52 North from Skegness (signposted for Ingoldmells) and continue for 3 miles. Turn left onto Walls Lane opposite the Butlins signposted for the Water Leisure Park. After ¼ mile turn left into the Park and follow the signs for the Railway.

Llanberis Lake Railway

Address: Gilfach Ddu, Llanberis, Gwynedd LL55 4TY
Telephone Nº: (01286) 870549
Year Formed: 1970
Location of Line: Just off the A4086 Caernarfon to Capel Curig road at Llanberis
Length of Line: 2½ miles
Nº of Steam Locos: 3
Nº of Other Locos: 4
Approx Nº of Visitors P.A.: 80,000
Gauge: 1 foot 11½ inches
Web site: www.lake-railway.co.uk

GENERAL INFORMATION

Nearest Mainline Station: Bangor (8 miles)
Nearest Bus Station: Caernarfon (6 miles) (there is a bus stop by Llanberis Station)
Car Parking: £3.00 Council car park on site
Coach Parking: Ample free parking on site
Souvenir Shop(s): Yes
Food & Drinks: Yes

SPECIAL INFORMATION

Llanberis Lake Railway runs along part of the trackbed of the Padarn Railway which transported slates for export and closed in 1961. An extension to Llanberis village opened in June 2003. The railway celebrates 40 years of service in 2011 with a special Gala to be held on 2nd and 3rd July.

OPERATING INFORMATION

Opening Times: 2011 dates: Open most days from mid-March to 29th October, daily from 22nd May to 2nd September and on certain days during the winter. Please send for a free timetable or check out the railway's web site.
Steam Working: Every operating day. Trains generally run from 11.00am to 4.00pm.
Prices: Adult £7.40
Child £4.50
Concessions £6.90
Family ticket £19.80 (2 Adult + 2 Children)
A range of other family discounts are also available.
Note: The Welsh Slate Museum is situated adjacent to the Railway.

Detailed Directions by Car:
The railway is situated just off the A4086 Caernarfon to Capel Curig road. Follow signs for Padarn Country Park.

Lynton & Barnstaple Railway

Address: Woody Bay Station, Martinhoe Cross, Parracombe, Devon EX31 4RA
Telephone Nº: (01598) 763487
Year Formed: 1993
Location of Line: North Devon
Length of Line: One mile

Nº of Steam Locos: 2
Nº of Other Locos: 1
Nº of Members: 2,200
Annual Membership Fee: £22.00
Approx Nº of Visitors P.A.: 35,000
Gauge: 1 foot 11½ inches
Web site: www.lynton-rail.co.uk

GENERAL INFORMATION

Nearest Mainline Station: Barnstaple
Nearest Bus Station: Barnstaple
Car Parking: Available at Woody Bay Station
Coach Parking: Available by prior arrangement
Souvenir Shop(s): Yes – at Woody Bay Station
Food & Drinks: Available at Woody Bay Station

SPECIAL INFORMATION

Passengers were first carried on a short stretch of this scenic narrow-gauge railway in July 2004. This was the first time the track had been used since the original railway closed in September 1935. The ultimate aim of the Lynton & Barnstaple Railway Trust is to re-open all 19 miles of the line.

OPERATING INFORMATION

Opening Times: Open most days from Easter until the end of October and selected dates in November and December. Please check with the railway for exact dates. Trains run from 10.30am to 4.30pm.
Steam Working: Most trains are steam-hauled except on Mondays and Fridays outside of the school holidays or in the event of breakdown.
Prices: Adult Return £7.00
Child Return £3.00 (Under-14s)
Senior Citizen Return £5.00
Family Ticket £18 (2 Adults + 3 Children)

Detailed Directions by Car:
From All Parts: Woody Bay Station is located alongside the A39 halfway between Lynton and Blackmoor Gate and one mile north-east of the village of Parracombe.

MARGAM PARK RAILWAY

Address: Margam Country Park, Port Talbot SA13 2TJ
Telephone Nº: (01639) 881635
Year Formed: 1976
Location of Line: Margam Country Park
Length of Line: 990 yards

Nº of Steam Locos: None
Nº of Other Locos: 1
Approx Nº of Visitors P.A.: 200,000 (to the Park itself)
Gauge: 2 feet
Web site: www.npt.gov.uk/margampark

GENERAL INFORMATION

Nearest Mainline Station: Port Talbot (3 miles)
Nearest Bus Station: Port Talbot (3 miles)
Car Parking: Available on site for a £3.50 charge
Coach Parking: Available
Souvenir Shop(s): Yes
Food & Drinks: Available

SPECIAL INFORMATION

Set in 1,000 acres of glorious parkland, Margam Country Park features an 18th Century Orangery, a Tudor-Gothic Victorian Mansion House and a 12th Century Chapter House.

OPERATING INFORMATION

Opening Times: 2011 dates: Daily from 2nd April to 4th September. Trains run from 10.00am to 5.00pm.
Steam Working: None at present
Prices: Adults £1.50
Children £1.00
Concessions £1.00
Family Ticket £4.00
(2 adults + 2 children)

Detailed Directions by Car:
From All Parts: Exit the M4 at Junction 38 and take the A48 towards Pyle following the brown tourist signs for Margam Country Park. The Park is situated on the left hand side of the road.

Markeaton Park Light Railway

Address: Markeaton Park, Derby, DE22
Telephone Nº: (01623) 552292
Year Formed: 1989
Location of Line: Markeaton Park
Length of Line: 1,400 yards
Web site: http://markeaton-park-light-railway.webs.com

Nº of Steam Locos: None
Nº of Other Locos: 1
Approx Nº of Visitors P.A.: Not known
Gauge: 15 inches

GENERAL INFORMATION

Nearest Mainline Station: Derby (2 miles)
Nearest Bus Station: Derby (2 miles)
Car Parking: Available adjacent to the railway
Coach Parking: Available
Souvenir Shop(s): None
Food & Drinks: Available

SPECIAL INFORMATION

Markeaton Park Light Railway opened in 1989 and after extensions in 1996 now runs from the main car park, over two major bridges to a second terminus adjacent to the play area at Mundy Halt.

OPERATING INFORMATION

Opening Times: During weekends and school holidays throughout the year with trains running hourly from 11.00am to 6.30pm during summer months and until 4.00pm during winter months.
Steam Working: None at present. Steam may return in the shape of visiting locomotives, namely the former resident engine , 'Markeaton Lady'.
Prices: Single £1.00 Return £2.00

Detailed Directions by Car:
Markeaton Park is situated in the North-West corner of Derby just to the North of the Junction between the A38 Queensway and A52 Ashbourne Road. The railway itself is situated adjacent to the main car park.

National Coal Mining Museum for England

Address: Caphouse Colliery, New Road, Overton, Wakefield WF4 4RH
Telephone Nº: (01924) 848806
Year Formed: 1988
Location of Line: West Yorkshire
Length of Line: 500 yards
Nº of Steam Locos: None in service
Nº of Other Locos: 2
Approx Nº of Visitors P.A.: 120,000 (to the Museum)
Gauge: 2 feet 6 inches
Web site: www.ncm.org.uk

GENERAL INFORMATION

Nearest Mainline Station: Wakefield (5 miles)
Nearest Bus Station: Wakefield (5 miles)
Car Parking: Available on site
Coach Parking: Available
Souvenir Shop(s): Yes
Food & Drinks: Available

SPECIAL INFORMATION

The National Coal Mining Museum for England offers an unusual combination of exciting experiences. The highlight of any visit is the underground tour where experienced local miners guide parties around the underground workings. Each visitor is provided with a hat, belt and battery, so that the true atmosphere of working life underground is captured. Above ground there are genuine pit ponies, a train ride, machinery displays, steam winder, pithead baths and the 42-acre rural site with its nature trail and adventure playground to be enjoyed. In addition, a modern visitor centre has been built with multimedia audio-visual displays, galleries and exhibitions, a licensed cafe and well-stocked shop.

OPERATING INFORMATION

Opening Times: Daily throughout the year except for Christmas Day, Boxing Day and New Year's Day. Open from 10.00am to 5.00pm.
Steam Working: None
Prices: Admission to the Museum is free of charge. Return train rides are £1.00 per person.

Detailed Directions by Car:
From All Parts: Take the M1 to Wakefield and follow the brown tourist signs for the National Coal Mining Museum which is at the side of the A642 in Overton.

North Bay Miniature Railway

Address: Burniston Road, Scarborough, YO12 6PF
Telephone Nº: (01723) 368791
Year Opened: 1931
Location: Peasholm Park to Scalby Mills
Length of Line: 1 mile
Nº of Steam Locos: None
Nº of Other Locos: 4
Nº of Members: None
Approx Nº of Visitors P.A.: 200,000
Gauge: 20 inches
Web site: www.nbr.org.uk

GENERAL INFORMATION

Nearest Mainline Station: Scarborough
Nearest Bus Station: Scarborough
Car Parking: Adjacent to the railway
Coach Parking: Adjacent to the railway
Souvenir Shop(s): Yes
Food & Drinks: Yes

SPECIAL INFORMATION

The North Bay Miniature Railway was opened in 1931 and operates between Northstead Manor and Scalby Mills for the Sea Life Centre.

OPERATING INFORMATION

Opening Times: Daily from 2nd April until the end of October then at weekends and local school holidays during the winter. Trains run at varying times, depending on the time of the year.
Please phone (01723) 368791 for further details.
Steam Working: None
Prices: Adult Return £3.10
Child Return £2.50

Detailed Directions by Car:
From All Parts: Take the A64, A165 or A170 to Scarborough and follow the signs for North Bay Leisure Park. The railway is situated just off the A165 opposite Peasholm Park. Alternatively, follow signs for the Sea Life Centre for Scalby Mills Station.

North Ings Farm Museum

Address: Fen Road, Dorrington, Lincoln LN4 3QB
Telephone N°: (01526) 833100
Year Formed: 1971
Location of Line: Dorrington
Length of Line: A third of a mile

N° of Steam Locos: 1
N° of Other Locos: 8
Approx N° of Visitors P.A.: Not recorded
Gauge: 2 feet
Website: www.northingsfarmmuseum.co.uk

GENERAL INFORMATION

Nearest Mainline Station: Ruskington (3 miles)
Nearest Bus Station: Dorrington (1 mile)
Car Parking: Free parking available on site
Coach Parking: Free parking available on site
Souvenir Shop(s): None
Food & Drinks: None

SPECIAL INFORMATION

The railway forms part of an agricultural machinery and tractor museum, originally built to serve the farm.

OPERATING INFORMATION

Opening Times: The first Sunday of the month from April through to October inclusive. Open from 10.00am to 5.00pm
Steam Working: Subject to availability. Please contact the Farm Museum for further information.
Prices: Adult £3.00
Child £1.50

Detailed Directions by Car:
From All Parts: North Ings Farm Museum is situated just off the B1188 between Lincoln and Sleaford. Turn into Dorrington Village at the Musician's Arms public house, pass through the village and under the railway bridge. The Museum entrance is on the right after 600 yards and the Museum is then ½ mile down the farm road.

Old Kiln Light Railway

Address: Rural Life Centre, Reeds Road, Tilford, Farnham, Surrey GU10 2DL
Telephone Nº: (01252) 795571
Year Formed: 1975
Location: 3 miles south of Farnham
Length of Line: ¾ mile **Gauge:** 2 feet
Nº of Steam Locos: 2
Nº of Other Locos: 10
Nº of Members: 14
Annual Membership Fee: £25.00
Approx Nº of Visitors P.A.: 21,000
Web site: www.oldkilnlightrailway.com

GENERAL INFORMATION

Nearest Mainline Station: Farnham (4 miles)
Nearest Bus Station: Farnham
Car Parking: Free parking available on site
Coach Parking: Free parking available on site
Souvenir Shop(s): Yes
Food & Drinks: Available

SPECIAL INFORMATION

The Railway is part of the Rural Life Centre at Tilford. The Centre contains the biggest country life collection in the South of England with a wide range of attractions. A line extension to ¾ mile has recently been opened.

OPERATING INFORMATION

Opening Times: 2011 dates: The Rural Life Centre is open Wednesday to Sunday and Bank Holidays from 9th March to 30th October 10.00am – 5.00pm. Open Wednesdays and Sundays only during the winter 11.00am – 4.00pm.
Steam Working: 2011 dates: 23rd April (Steam Toy Rally), 30th April (Model Railway Exhibition), 7th & 8th May (A Village at War), 29th May (Tilford Bus & Coach Rally), 31st July (Rustic Sunday), 3rd & 4th September (Weyfest), 11th September (Donkey Day Out), 18th September (Classic Vehicle Gathering), 24th & 25th September (Steam & Vintage Weekend), 10, 11th, 17th & 18th December (Santa Specials)
Prices: Steam-hauled rides £1.50
Diesel-hauled rides £1.00

Detailed Directions by Car:
The Rural Life Centre is situated 3 miles south of Farnham. From Farnham take the A287 southwards before turning left at Millbridge crossroads into Reeds Road. The Centre is on the left after about ½ mile, just after the Frensham Garden Centre; From the A3: Turn off at the Hindhead crossroads and head north to Tilford. Pass through Tilford, cross the River Wey then turn left into Reeds Road. The Centre is on the right after ½ mile.

PERRYGROVE RAILWAY

Address: Perrygrove Railway, Coleford, Gloucestershire GL16 8QB
Telephone Nº: (01594) 834991
Year Formed: 1996
Location of Line: ½ mile south of Coleford
Length of Line: ¾ mile

Nº of Steam Locos: 4
Nº of Other Locos: 2
Nº of Members: 6
Approx Nº of Visitors P.A.: 20,000
Gauge: 15 inches
Web site: www.perrygrove.co.uk

GENERAL INFORMATION

Nearest Mainline Station: Lydney (for Parkend)
Nearest Bus Station: Bus stops in Coleford
Car Parking: Free parking available on site
Coach Parking: Free parking on site
Souvenir Shop(s): Yes
Food & Drinks: Sandwiches & light refreshments are available

SPECIAL INFORMATION

Perrygrove is a unique railway with 4 stations, all with access to private woodland walks. Lots of picnic tables are available in the open and under cover. There is also an indoor village with secret passages, a play area and a new Treetop Adventure.
The train fare includes admission to all attractions.

OPERATING INFORMATION

Opening Times: Every Saturday, Sunday and Bank Holiday from late March to November and daily throughout the local school holidays. Santa Specials also run (pre-booking is essential for these). Please phone for further details. Railway opens at 10.30am with the last train at 4.15pm or 3.45pm depending on the time of year.
Steam Working: Most services are steam-hauled and driver experience courses are also available.
Prices: Adult £6.20 (All-day ticket)
Senior Citizen £5.70 (All-day ticket)
Child (ages 3-16) £4.80 (All-day ticket)

Detailed Directions by Car:
From All Parts: Travel to Coleford, Gloucestershire. Upon reaching the vicinity of Coleford, the Perrygrove Railway is clearly signposted with brown tourist signs from all directions.

POOLE PARK RAILWAY

Address: Poole Park, Parkstone Road, Poole BH15 1SR
Telephone Nº: 07947 846262
Year Formed: 1949
Location of Line: Poole, Dorset
Length of Line: 1,100 yards
Nº of Steam Locos: 1
Nº of Other Locos: 2
Approx Nº of Visitors P.A.: 69,000
Gauge: 10¼ inches
Web site: www.pooleparktrains.co.uk

GENERAL INFORMATION

Nearest Mainline Station: Poole (½ mile)
Nearest Bus Station: Poole (¼ mile)
Car Parking: Available on site
Coach Parking: Available
Souvenir Shop(s): Yes
Food & Drinks: Available

SPECIAL INFORMATION

The railways circumnavigates a wildfowl lake which is home to wide variety of ducks, geese and swans.

OPERATING INFORMATION

Opening Times: 2011 dates: Daily from 1st March to 5th January (2012) then weekends and during January and February. Open from 10.00am to 5.00pm.
Steam Working: School Holidays and weekends from 1st July 2011
Prices: Adults £1.40
Children £1.40

Detailed Directions by Car:
From All Parts: Take the A31 then the A348 to Poole and follow the brown tourist signs for Poole Park.

Queen's Park Miniature Railway

Address: Queen's Park, Boythorpe Road, Chesterfield S40 2BF
Telephone N°: (01246) 345777
Year Formed: 1976
Location of Line:
Length of Line: 550 yards

N° of Steam Locos: None
N° of Other Locos: 1
Approx N° of Visitors P.A.: 350,000 (to the Park itself)
Gauge: 10¼ inches
Web site: www.chesterfield.gov.uk/default.aspx?CATID=761&CID=4097

GENERAL INFORMATION

Nearest Mainline Station: Chesterfield (1 mile)
Nearest Bus Station: Chesterfield (¼ mile)
Car Parking: Available on site
Coach Parking: Available
Souvenir Shop(s): None
Food & Drinks: Available

SPECIAL INFORMATION

The railway runs through a 22-acre Green Flag listed park which was opened in 1887 to commemorate Queen Victoria's Golden Jubilee.

OPERATING INFORMATION

Opening Times: Daily from Easter to the end of September, from 11.00am to 5.00pm.
Steam Working: None
Prices: Adults £1.60
Children £1.60 (Free for Under-3s)

Detailed Directions by Car:
From All Parts: Exit the M1 at Junction 29 and take the A617 into Chesterfield. Turn left at the 2nd roundabout following signs for Matlock/Buxton and then left onto the A632 at the next roundabout signposted for Matlock. The Park is on the right after approximately 200 yards.

Ravenglass & Eskdale Railway

Address: Ravenglass, Cumbria
CA18 1SW
Telephone Nº: (01229) 717171
Year Formed: 1875
Location: The Lake District National Park
Length of Line: 7 miles

Gauge: 15 inches
Nº of Steam Locos: 6
Nº of Other Locos: 8
Nº of Members: None
Approx Nº of Visitors P.A.: 120,000
Web site: www.ravenglass-railway.co.uk
E-mail: steam@ravenglass-railway.co.uk

GENERAL INFORMATION

Nearest Mainline Station: Ravenglass (adjacent)
Nearest Bus Stop: Ravenglass
Car Parking: Available at both terminals
Coach Parking: At Ravenglass
Souvenir Shop(s): Yes
Food & Drinks: Yes

SPECIAL INFORMATION

From Ravenglass, the Lake District's only coastal village, the line runs through two lovely valleys to the foot of England's highest mountain. A new station and visitor centre featuring Fellbites eatery, Scafell Gift Shop and the Eskdale Meeting Room is now open at Dalegarth (Eskdale). A new cafe opens at Ravenglass in time for Easter 2011.

OPERATING INFORMATION

Opening Times: 2011 dates: The service runs daily from the 2nd April until the 30th October inclusive. Trains also run during most weekends in the Winter, around Christmas and at February half-term. Open from 9.00am to 5.00pm (sometimes later during high season).
Steam Working: Most services are steam hauled.
Prices: Adult £12.00
Child £6.00 (Ages 5 to 15)
Under-5s travel free

Detailed Directions by Car:
The railway is situated just off the main A595 Western Lake District road.

Rhyl Miniature Railway

Address: Marine Lake, Wellington Road, Rhyl LL18 1LN
Telephone Nº: (01352) 759109
Year Formed: 1911
Location of Line: Rhyl
Length of Line: 1 mile
Nº of Steam Locos: 5
Nº of Other Locos: 3
Nº of Members: Approximately 80
Annual Membership Fee: £7.50
Approx Nº of Visitors P.A.: 10,000
Gauge: 15 inches
Web site: www.rhylminiaturerailway.co.uk

GENERAL INFORMATION

Nearest Mainline Station: Rhyl (1 mile)
Nearest Bus Station: Rhyl (1 mile)
Car Parking: Car Park near the Railway
Coach Parking: Available nearby
Souvenir Shop(s): Yes
Food & Drinks: Available

SPECIAL INFORMATION

The trust runs the oldest Miniature Railway in the UK. From 28th to 30th May 2011, the railway will be holding a Centenary Gala with a host of attractions for the family. The principal locomotive and train have been operating there since the 1920's.

OPERATING INFORMATION

Opening Times: Every weekend from Easter until the end of September. Also on Bank Holiday Mondays and daily during the School Summer Holidays. Trains run from 11.00am to 4.00pm.
Steam Working: Every Sunday and also Thursday to Saturday during the School Summer Holidays.
Prices: Adult £2.00
Child £1.50

Detailed Directions by Car:
From All Parts: The Railway is located behind the west end of Rhyl Promenade.

Rio Grande Miniature Railway

Address: Saville Bros Garden Centre, Selby Road, Garforth, Leeds LS25 2AQ
Telephone Nº: (0113) 286-2183
Year Formed: 1978
Location of Line: A63 Garforth to Selby
Length of Line: ½ mile

Nº of Steam Locos: None
Nº of Other Locos: 1
Approx Nº of Visitors P.A.: 10,500
Gauge: 10¼ inches
Web site: www.klondyke.co.uk

GENERAL INFORMATION

Nearest Mainline Station: Garforth
Nearest Bus Station: Garforth
Car Parking: Available on site
Coach Parking: Available on site
Souvenir Shop(s): No
Food & Drinks: Café on site

SPECIAL INFORMATION

The Rio Grande Train, owned by William Strike Ltd. operates at the Saville Bros. Garden Centre.

OPERATING INFORMATION

Opening Times: Weekends and Bank Holidays from March to September. Trains run from 10.00am to 4.30pm.
Steam Working: None
Prices: Adult Return £1.00
Child Return £1.00

Detailed Directions by Car:
From the M1 and M62: Take the A1(M) north and exit at Junction 46. Follow the A63 towards Selby and go straight on at the next roundabout with the Old George Pub on the left. Continue straight on up the hill passing the Crusader pub on the left and the Garden Centre is on the left; From the A1: Exit the A1 onto the A63 (Milford Lodge Hotel) and follow signs towards Leeds. Go straight on at the first roundabout and the Garden Centre is on the right after approximately ½ mile.

Romney, Hythe & Dymchurch Railway

Address: New Romney Station,
New Romney, Kent TN28 8PL
Telephone Nº: (01797) 362353
Year Formed: 1927
Location of Line: Approximately 5 miles west of Folkestone
Length of Line: 13½ miles

Nº of Steam Locos: 11
Nº of Other Locos: 5
Nº of Members: 2,500
Annual Membership Fee: Supporters association – Adult £19.00; Junior £7.50
Approx Nº of Visitors P.A.: 160,000
Gauge: 15 inches
Web site: www.rhdr.org.uk

GENERAL INFORMATION

Nearest Mainline Station: Folkestone Central (5 miles) or Rye
Nearest Bus Station: Folkestone (then take bus to Hythe)
Car Parking: Free parking at all major stations
Coach Parking: At New Romney & Dungeness
Souvenir Shop(s): Yes – 4 at various stations
Food & Drinks: 2 Cafes serving food and drinks

SPECIAL INFORMATION

Opened in 1927 as 'The World's Smallest Public Railway'. Now the only 15" gauge tourist main line railway in the world. Double track, 6 stations.

OPERATING INFORMATION

Opening Times: 2011 dates: A daily service runs from 26th March to 30th October. Open at weekends in February, March and for Santa Specials during December. Also open daily during School half-terms.
Steam Working: All operational days.
Prices: Depend on length of journey. Maximum fares: Adult £15.00
Child £7.50
Family £39.50 (2 adults + 2 children)

Detailed Directions by Car:
Exit the M20 at Junction 11 then follow signs to Hythe and the brown tourist signs for the railway. Alternatively, Take the A259 to New Romney and follow the brown tourist signs for the railway.

Royal Victoria Railway

Address: Royal Victoria Country Park, Netley, Southampton SO31 5GA
Telephone Nº: (023) 8045-6246
Year Formed: 1995
Location of Line: Netley
Length of Line: 1 mile

Nº of Steam Locos: 10
Nº of Other Locos: 9
Approx Nº of Visitors P.A.: Not known
Gauge: 10¼ inches
Web site: www.royalvictoriarailway.co.uk

GENERAL INFORMATION

Nearest Mainline Station: Netley
Nearest Bus Station: Southampton
Car Parking: Available on site – £2.00 fee
Coach Parking: Free parking available on site
Souvenir Shop(s): Yes
Food & Drinks: Yes

SPECIAL INFORMATION

The railway runs through the grounds of an old Victorian hospital and has good views of the Solent and the Isle of Wight. The Park covers 200 acres including woodland, grassland, beaches, picnic sites and a play area.

OPERATING INFORMATION

Opening Times: Weekends throughout the year and daily during local school holidays. Trains run from 11.00am to 4.30pm. The railway also opens by appointment for larger parties.
Steam Working: On special event days only. Please phone for further details.
Prices: Adult Return £1.75
Child Return £1.25
Note: Special rates are available for groups of 10 or more when pre-booked. Under-2s travel free.

Detailed Directions by Car:
From All Parts: Exit the M27 at Junction 8 and follow the Brown Tourist signs for the Royal Victoria Country Park. You will reach the Park after approximately 3 miles.

Rudyard Lake Steam Railway

Address: Rudyard Station, Rudyard, Near Leek, Staffordshire ST13 8PF
Telephone Nº: (01538) 306704
Year Formed: 1985
Location: Rudyard to Hunthouse Wood
Length of Line: 1½ miles
Nº of Steam Locos: 5
Nº of Other Locos: 3
Approx Nº of Visitors P.A.: 50,000
Gauge: 10¼ inches and 7¼ inches
Web site: www.rlsr.org

GENERAL INFORMATION

Nearest Mainline Station: Stoke-on-Trent (10 miles)
Nearest Bus Station: Leek
Car Parking: Free parking at Rudyard Station
Coach Parking: Free parking at Rudyard Station
Souvenir Shop(s): Yes
Food & Drinks: Yes – Cafe open at weekends

SPECIAL INFORMATION

The Railway runs along the side of the historic Rudyard Lake that gave author Rudyard Kipling his name. A Steamboat also plies the lake at times. "Drive a Steam Train" courses can be booked or bought as a gift with vouchers valid for 9 months. A short 7¼ inch gauge railway operates on special event days.

OPERATING INFORMATION

Opening Times: 2011 dates: Every Sunday and Bank Holiday from January to the end of November. Also open on every Saturday from 26th March to 29th October and Monday to Friday from 18th to 29th April, 28th May to 5th June, 20th July to 4th September and 24th to 30th October. Santa Specials run on 10th and 11th December and there is a Steam Gala on 10th and 11th September.
Steam Working: All trains are normally steam hauled. Trains run from 11.00am and the last train runs around 4.00pm.
Prices: Adult Return £3.50
Child Return £2.50
A variety of other fares and Day Rover tickets are also available.

Detailed Directions by Car:
From All Parts: Head for Leek then follow the A523 North towards Macclesfield for 1 mile. Follow the brown tourist signs to the B5331 signposted for Rudyard for ½ mile. Pass under the Railway bridge and turn immediately left and go up the ramp to the Station car park.

Ruislip Lido Railway

Address: Reservoir Road, Ruislip, Middlesex HA4 7TY
Telephone Nº: (01895) 622595
Year Formed: 1979
Location of Line: Trains travel from Ruislip Lido to Woody Bay
Length of Line: 1¼ miles

Nº of Steam Locos: 1
Nº of Other Locos: 5
Nº of Members: 155
Annual Membership Fee: £15.00
Approx Nº of Visitors P.A.: 60,000
Gauge: 12 inches
Web site: www.ruisliplidorailway.org

Photo courtesy of Peter Musgrave

GENERAL INFORMATION

Nearest Mainline Station: West Ruislip (2 miles)
Nearest Bus Station: Ruislip Underground Station
Car Parking: Free parking available at the Lido
Coach Parking: Free parking available at the Lido
Souvenir Shop(s): Yes
Food & Drinks: A Beach Cafe is open on weekends and Bank Holidays. A Pub/Restaurant is open daily.

SPECIAL INFORMATION

The steam locomotive, 'Mad Bess' used by Ruislip Lido Railway was actually built by the members over a 12 year period!

OPERATING INFORMATION

Opening Times: Weekends from 9th February to 9th April and daily from 10th April to 2nd May and from 24th July to 11th September (during school holidays). Also open on weekends from September to November and on Sundays in December.
Steam Working: Sundays and Bank Holidays from July to the end of September and also Santa Specials.
Prices: Adult Return £2.50 (Single fare £2.00)
Child Return £2.00 (Single fare £1.50)
Family Return £7.50 (Single fare £6.00)
(2 adults + 2 children)
Note: Under-3s travel for free

Detailed Directions by Car:
From All Parts: Follow the signs from the A40 and take the A4180 through Ruislip before turning left onto the B469.

Saltburn Miniature Railway

Address: Valley Gardens, Saltburn
Correspondence: 55 High Street West, Redcar TS10 1SF
Telephone Nº: (01642) 502863
Year Formed: 1947
Location of Line: Cat Nab to Forest Halt Stations, Saltburn
Length of Line: ¾ mile

Nº of Steam Locos: Visiting locos only
Nº of Other Locos: 3
Nº of Members: 12
Annual Membership Fee: £1.00
Approx Nº of Visitors P.A.: 20,000
Gauge: 15 inches
Web site: www.saltburn-miniature-railway.org.uk

GENERAL INFORMATION

Nearest Mainline Station: Saltburn (½ mile)
Nearest Bus Station: Saltburn (½ mile)
Car Parking: Available at Cat Nab Station
Coach Parking: Glen Side (at the top of the bank)
Souvenir Shop(s): At Cat Nab Station
Food & Drinks: None

OPERATING INFORMATION

Opening Times: Weekends and Bank Holidays from Easter until the end of September. Also open Tuesday to Friday during the Summer School Holidays. Trains run from 1.00pm to 5.00pm.
Steam Working: Please contact the railway for details.
Prices: Adult Return £2.00 (Adult Single £1.00)
Child Return 1.00 (Child Single 50p)
Note: Family tickets and frequent user discounts are also available.

Detailed Directions by Car:
Follow the A174 from Middlesbrough (West) or Whitby (East) to Saltburn-by-the-Sea. Cat Nab Station with its adjoining car park is situated by the beach, directly off the A174 (C174).

Sherwood Forest Railway

Address: Gorsethorpe Lane, Edwinstowe, Mansfield NG21 9HL
Telephone Nº: (01623) 515339
Year Formed: 1999
Location of Line: Between Mansfield Woodhouse and Edwinstowe
Length of Line: 680 yards
Nº of Steam Locos: 2
Nº of Other Locos: 3
Nº of Members: 13
Annual Membership Fee: –
Approx Nº of Visitors P.A.: 17,000
Gauge: 15 inches
Web site: www.sherwoodforestrailway.com

GENERAL INFORMATION

Nearest Mainline Station: Mansfield (7 miles)
Nearest Bus Station: Mansfield (7 miles)
Car Parking: Free parking available on site
Coach Parking: Available on site
Souvenir Shop(s): Yes
Food & Drinks: Available

SPECIAL INFORMATION

The Railway runs through the grounds of a former 26 acre Farm Park which has play areas for children and picnic areas.

OPERATING INFORMATION

Opening Times: 2011 dates: Weekends and Bank Holidays through the year and daily during the school holidays. Trains run from 11.00am to 5.00pm on most days but from 10.00am on Bank Holidays.
Steam Working: Every operating day
Prices: Adults £1.00 (Allows rides for a day)
Chidren £1.00 (Allows rides for a day)
Family £4.00 (Allows rides for a day)

Detailed Directions by Car:
From the A1: Turn off at the Worksop roundabout and head to Ollerton. Follow the A6075 through Edwinstowe and towards Mansfield Woodhouse, then turn left at the double mini-roundabout. The Farm Park is on the right after approximately 200 yards; From Nottingham: Head to Ollerton, then as above; From the M1: Exit at Junction 27 and head into Mansfield. Follow signs to Mansfield Woodhouse and then on towards Edwinstowe. From here, follow the tourist signs for the Farm Park.

SHIBDEN MINIATURE RAILWAY

Address: Shibden Park, Listers Lane, Halifax HX3 6XG
Telephone Nº: 07854 658635
Year Formed: 1983
Location of Line: Halifax, West Yorkshire
Length of Line: ½ miles

Nº of Steam Locos: 1
Nº of Other Locos: 1
Approx Nº of Visitors P.A.: Not known
Gauge: 10¼ inches
E-mail: shibdenrailway@hotmail.com

GENERAL INFORMATION

Nearest Mainline Station: Halifax (2 miles)
Nearest Bus Station: Halifax (2 miles)
Car Parking: Available on site
Coach Parking: Available
Souvenir Shop(s): None
Food & Drinks: Available in the Park

SPECIAL INFORMATION

The railway operates in the public park surrounding Shibden Hall, a historic house which dates back to around 1420.

OPERATING INFORMATION

Opening Times: Weekends throughout the year and daily during the School Holidays from 11.00am to 5.00pm, weather permitting.
Steam Working: Sundays and Bank Holidays, subject to the weather.
Prices: Adults £1.20
Children £1.20

Detailed Directions by Car:
From All Parts: Exit the M62 at Junction 25 and take the A644 to Hipperholme then follow the A58 towards Halifax. The Park is on the left of the A58 as you enter Halifax and is well-signposted.

Snowdon Mountain Railway

Address: Llanberis, Caernarfon, Gwynedd, Wales LL55 4TY
Telephone Nº: 0844 493-8120
Fax Nº: (01286) 872518
Year Formed: 1894
Location of Line: Llanberis to the summit of Snowdon
Length of Line: 4¾ miles
Nº of Steam Locos: 4
Nº of Other Locos: 4
Approx Nº of Visitors P.A.: 140,000
Gauge: 2 feet 7½ inches
Web site: www.snowdonrailway.co.uk

GENERAL INFORMATION

Nearest Mainline Station: Bangor (9 miles)
Nearest Bus Station: Caernarfon (7½ miles)
Car Parking: Llanberis Station car park – pay and display. Also other car parks nearby.
Coach Parking: As above but space is very limited
Souvenir Shop(s): Yes
Food & Drinks: Yes

SPECIAL INFORMATION

Britain's only public rack and pinion railway climbs to within 60 feet of the 3,560 feet peak of Snowdon, the highest mountain in England and Wales. The return journet to the summit takes approximately 2½ hours which includes a 30 minute stop at the peak. The new Snowdon Summit Visitor Centre, Hafod Eryri is now open.

OPERATING INFORMATION

Opening Times: 2011 dates: Open daily (weather permitting) from 19th March to 30th October. Trains run every 30 minutes (subject to public demand) from 9.00am until mid/late afternoon. The last departure can be as late as 5.00pm depending on demand. It is advisable to guarantee tickets and book in advance either on-line or by telephone.
Steam Working: Trains may be operated by either steam or diesel depending on engine availability.
Prices: Adult Summit Return £25.00
Child Summit Return £18.00
Special rates are available for large groups. Please phone 0844 493-8120 for further details.

Detailed Directions by Car:
Llanberis Station is situated on the A4086 Caernarfon to Capel Curig road, 7½ miles from Caernarfon. Convenient access via the main North Wales coast road (A55). Exit at the A55/A5 junction and follow signs to Llanberis via B4366, B4547 and A4086.

South Downs Light Railway

Address: South Downs Light Railway, Stopham Road, Pulborough RH20 1DS
Telephone Nº: 07518 753784
Year Formed: 1999
Location: Pulborough Garden Centre
Length of Line: 1 kilometre

Nº of Steam Locos: 10
Nº of Other Locos: 2
Nº of Members: 60
Annual Membership Fee: Adult £20.00
Approx Nº of Visitors P.A.: 15,000
Gauge: 10¼ inches
Web site: www.sdlrs.com

GENERAL INFORMATION

Nearest Mainline Station: Pulborough (½ mile)
Nearest Bus Station: Bus stop just outside Centre
Car Parking: Free parking on site
Coach Parking: Free parking on site
Souvenir Shop(s): Yes
Food & Drinks: Yes – in the Garden Restaurant

SPECIAL INFORMATION

The members of the Society own and operate the largest collection of 10¼ inch gauge scale locomotives in the UK. The Railway is sited in the Wyevale Garden Centre.

OPERATING INFORMATION

Opening Times: Weekends and Bank Holidays from March until September, Wednesdays in August and also Santa Specials at weekends in December. Trains run from 11.00am to 3.30pm.
Steam Working: Most services are steam hauled.
Prices: Adult £1.50
Child £1.00 (Under-2s travel free of charge)
Note: Supersaver tickets are also available.

Detailed Directions by Car:
From All Parts: The Centre is situated on the A283, ½ mile west of Pulborough. Pulborough itself is on the A29 London to Bognor Regis Road.

SOUTHEND PIER RAILWAY

Address: Western Esplanade, Southend-on-Sea SS1 1EE
Telephone Nº: (01702) 618747
Year Formed: 1889
Location of Line: Southend seafront
Length of Line: 2,180 yards
Nº of Steam Locos: None
Nº of Other Locos: 2
Approx Nº of Visitors P.A.: 300,000
Gauge: 3 feet
Web site: www.southend.gov.uk/content.asp?section=583

GENERAL INFORMATION

Nearest Mainline Station: Southend Central (¼ mile)
Nearest Bus Station: Southend (¼ mile)
Car Parking: Available on the seafront
Coach Parking: Available
Souvenir Shop(s): Yes
Food & Drinks: Available

SPECIAL INFORMATION

The railway takes passengers to the end of Southend Pier which, at 1.33 miles, is the longest pleasure pier in the world.

OPERATING INFORMATION

Opening Times: Daily except for Christmas Day. Times vary depending on the season – trains run from 8.30am to 7.00pm during the Summer.
Steam Working: None.
Prices: Adult Return £3.58
Child Return £1.79
Concessionary Return £1.79
Family Return Ticket £8.68

Detailed Directions by Car:
From All Parts: Take the A127 to Southend and follow the brown tourist signs to the Pier.

South Tynedale Railway

Address: The Railway Station, Alston, Cumbria CA9 3JB
Telephone Nº: (01434) 381696 (Enquiries) (01434) 382828 (Talking timetable)
Year Formed: 1973
Location of Line: From Alston, northwards along South Tyne Valley to Kirkhaugh
Length of Line: 2¼ miles
Nº of Steam Locos: 5
Nº of Other Locos: 5
Nº of Members: 290
Annual Membership Fee: £16.00
Approx Nº of Visitors P.A.: 22,000
Gauge: 2 feet
Web site: www.strps.org.uk

GENERAL INFORMATION

Nearest Mainline Station: Haltwhistle (15 miles)
Nearest Bus Station: Alston Townfoot (¼ mile)
Car Parking: Free parking at Alston Station
Coach Parking: Free parking at Alston Station
Souvenir Shop(s): Yes
Food & Drinks: Yes

OPERATING INFORMATION

Opening Times: 2011 dates: Bank Holidays and Weekends from 22nd April until the end of October. Open daily from 16th July to 31st August. Also open Tuesdays and Thursdays in June and September. Please contact the Railway for further details.
Steam Working: Varies, but generally weekends and Bank Holidays throughout Summer & December.
Prices: Adult Return £6.00; Adult Single £4.00
Child Return £3.00; Child Single £2.00
Family Return Ticket £16.50
Children under 3 travel free
Adult All Day Ticket £10.00
Child All Day Ticket £5.00

Detailed Directions by Car:
Alston can be reached by a number of roads from various directions including A689, A686 and the B6277. Alston Station is situated just off the A686 Hexham road, north of Alston Town Centre. Look for the brown tourist signs on roads into Alston.

St. Annes Miniature Railway

Address: Seafront, St. Annes-on-Sea, Lancashire
Telephone Nº: (01772) 864875
Year Formed: 1973
Location of Line: St. Annes seafront
Length of Line: 700 yards
Nº of Steam Locos: None
Nº of Other Locos: 2
Approx Nº of Visitors P.A.: 6,000
Gauge: 10¼ inches
Web site: None

GENERAL INFORMATION

Nearest Mainline Station: St. Annes (¾ mile)
Nearest Bus Station: Blackpool (3 miles)
Car Parking: Available on site
Coach Parking: Available
Souvenir Shop(s): None
Food & Drinks: Available

SPECIAL INFORMATION

This rectangular line runs through the sand dunes on the St. Annes seafront.

OPERATING INFORMATION

Opening Times: Daily from Easter until the end of September, from 11.00am to 5.00pm.
Steam Working: None.
Prices: £1.80 per ride

Detailed Directions by Car:
From All Parts: Exit the M55 at Junction 4 and follow the A5230 then the A584 to St. Annes. The railway is located on the seafront next to Pleasure Island.

Steeple Grange Light Railway

Address: High Peak Trail, Near National Stone Centre, Wirksworth DE4 4LS	**Nº of Steam Locos:** 1 (awaiting rebuild)
Telephone Nº: (01629) 580917	**Nº of Other Locos:** 17
Operating Day Contact Nº: 07769 802587	**Nº of Members:** 200
Year Formed: 1986	**Annual Membership Fee:** From £6.00
Location of Line: Off the High Peak trail near Wirksworth	**Approx Nº of Visitors P.A.:** 8,000+
Length of Line: ½ mile at present	**Gauge:** 18 inches
	Web site: www.steeplegrange.co.uk

GENERAL INFORMATION

Nearest Mainline Station: Cromford (2 miles)
Nearest Bus Station: Matlock
Car Parking: Free parking available nearby
Coach Parking: Free parking available nearby
Souvenir Shop(s): Yes
Food & Drinks: Light refreshments available

SPECIAL INFORMATION

The Railway is built on the track bed of the former Standard Gauge Cromford and High Peak Railway branch to Middleton. The railway uses mostly former mining/quarrying rolling stock and has two separate lines operating.

OPERATING INFORMATION

Opening Times: Sundays and Bank Holidays from Easter until the end of October. Also open on Saturdays from July to September and by prior arrangement. Special Events at other times of the year including Santa Specials on dates in December. Please contact the railway for further details.
Trains run from 12.00pm to 5.00pm
Steam Working: None at present
Prices: Adult Return £2.00
Child Return £1.00
Family Return £5.00
Note: Special fares apply during special events and also for group bookings.

Detailed Directions by Car:
The Railway is situated adjacent to the National Stone Centre just to the north of Wirksworth at the junction of the B5035 and B5036. Free car parking is available at the National Stone Centre and in Old Porter Lane.

Sutton Hall Railway

Address: Tabors Farm, Sutton Hall, Shopland Road, near Rochford, Essex SS4 1LQ	**Nº of Steam Locos:** 1
Telephone Nº: (01702) 334337	**Nº of Other Locos:** 1
Year Formed: 1997	**Nº of Members:** Approximately 8
Location of Line: Sutton Hall Farm	**Annual Membership Fee:** £15.00
Length of Line: Almost 1 mile	**Approx Nº of Visitors P.A.:** 3,500
	Gauge: 10¼ inches
	Web site: None at present

GENERAL INFORMATION

Nearest Mainline Station: Rochford (1½ miles)
Nearest Bus Station: Rochford
Car Parking: Free parking available on site
Coach Parking: Free parking available on site
Souvenir Shop(s): None
Food & Drinks: Drinks and snacks available

SPECIAL INFORMATION

The Railway was bought by C. Tabor in 1985 for use with his Farm Barn Dances. The Sutton Hall Railway Society was formed in 1997 (with C. Tabor as Society President) and now opens the line for public running on some Sundays. The railway is staffed entirely by Volunteer Members of the Society.

OPERATING INFORMATION

Opening Times: Open the 4th Sunday in the month from April until September, 12.00pm to 6.00pm. Specials run on Easter Sunday afternoon, Halloween evening (5.00pm to 10.00pm) and a Santa Special on the afternoon of the first Sunday in December (12.00pm to 5.00pm).
Steam Working: All operating days.
Prices: Adult Return £2.00
Child Return £1.50

Detailed Directions by Car:
From Southend Airport (A127 Southend to London Main Route & A1159): At the Airport Roundabout (with the McDonalds on the left) go over the railway bridge signposted for Rochford. At the 1st roundabout turn right (Ann Boleyn Pub on the right) into Sutton Road. Continue straight on at the mini-roundabout then when the road forks turn left into Shopland Road signposted for Barling and Great Wakering. Turn right after approximately 400 yards into the long tree-lined road for Sutton Hall Farm.

TALYLLYN RAILWAY

Address: Wharf Station, Tywyn, Gwynedd, LL36 9EY
Telephone Nº: (01654) 710472
Year Formed: 1865
Location of Line: Tywyn to Nant Gwernol Station
Length of Line: 7¼ miles
Nº of Steam Locos: 6
Nº of Other Locos: 4
Nº of Members: 3,500
Annual Membership Fee: Adult £25.00
Approx Nº of Visitors P.A.: 50,000
Gauge: 2 feet 3 inches
Web site: www.talyllyn.co.uk

GENERAL INFORMATION

Nearest Mainline Station: Tywyn (300 yards)
Nearest Bus Station: Tywyn (300 yards)
Car Parking: 100 yards away
Coach Parking: Free parking (100 yards)
Souvenir Shop(s): Yes
Food & Drinks: Yes

SPECIAL INFORMATION

Talyllyn Railway was the first preserved railway in the world – saved from closure in 1951. The railway was originally opened in 1866 to carry slate from Bryn Eglwys Quarry to Tywyn. Among the railway's attractions are a Narrow Gauge Railway Museum at the Tywyn Wharf terminus.

OPERATING INFORMATION

Opening Times: 2011 dates: Daily from 2nd April to 30th October and on other delected dates if February, March, November and December. Generally open from 10.00am to 5.00pm (later during the summer). Please contact the railway or check the web site for further details.
Steam Working: All services are steam-hauled.
Prices: Adult Return £13.00 (Day Rover ticket)
Senior Citizen Return £11.50
Children (ages 5-15) pay £3.00 if travelling with an adult. Otherwise, they pay half adult fare. Children under the age of 5 travel free of charge.
Family ticket (one child) £28.00
Family ticket (two children) £31.00
Single and shorter journeys are cheaper.

Detailed Directions by Car:
From the North: Take the A493 from Dolgellau into Tywyn; From the South: Take the A493 from Machynlleth to Tywyn.

Teifi Valley Railway

Address: Henllan Station, Henllan, near Newcastle Emlyn, Carmarthenshire
Telephone Nº: (01559) 371077
Year Formed: 1978
Location of Line: Between Cardigan and Carmarthen off the A484
Length of Line: 2 miles
Nº of Steam Locos: 2
Nº of Other Locos: 3
Nº of Members: Approximately 150
Annual Membership Fee: £12.00
Approx Nº of Visitors P.A.: 15,000
Gauge: 2 feet
Web site: www.teifivalleyrailway.com

GENERAL INFORMATION

Nearest Mainline Station: Carmarthen (10 miles)
Nearest Bus Station: Carmarthen (10 miles)
Car Parking: Spaces for 70 cars available.
Coach Parking: Spaces for 4 coaches available.
Souvenir Shop(s): Yes
Food & Drinks: Yes (snacks only)

SPECIAL INFORMATION

The Railway was formerly part of the G.W.R. but now runs on a Narrow Gauge using Quarry Engines.

OPERATING INFORMATION

Opening Times: 2011 dates: Open daily from 17th April to 5th May (plus some other dates in April and May) then 29th May to 29th September (closed on some Fridays and Saturdays in June, July and September). Open daily from 23rd to 29th October and on 10th, 11th, 17th, 18th and 22nd to 24th December for 'Santa Specials'. Trains run from 11.30am to either 3.00pm or 4.00pm.
Steam Working: Most operating days – please phone the Railway for further details.
Prices: Adult £6.00 Child £4.00
Senior Citizen £5.50
A 10% discount is available for parties of 10 or more.

Detailed Directions by Car:
From All Parts: The Railway is situated in the Village of Henllan between the A484 and the A475 (on the B4334) about 4 miles east of Newcastle Emlyn.

TODDINGTON NARROW GAUGE RAILWAY

Address: The Station, Toddington, Cheltenham, Gloucestershire GL54 5DT
Telephone N°: (01242) 621405
Year Formed: 1985
Location of Line: 5 miles south of Broadway, Worcestershire, near the A46
Length of Line: ½ mile
N° of Steam Locos: 3
N° of Other Locos: 5
N° of Members: Approximately 35
Annual Membership Fee: £6.00
Approx N° of Visitors P.A.: 2,000
Gauge: 2 feet
Web site: www.toddington-narrow-gauge.co.uk

GENERAL INFORMATION

Nearest Mainline Station: Cheltenham Spa or Ashchurch
Nearest Bus Station: Cheltenham
Car Parking: Parking available at Toddington, Winchcombe & Cheltenham Racecourse Stations
Coach Parking: Parking available as above
Souvenir Shop(s): None
Food & Drinks: None at the TNGR itself but available at the adjacent GWSR site.

SPECIAL INFORMATION

The railway boasts the only German-built World War One Henschel locomotive in this country.

OPERATING INFORMATION

Opening Times: 2011 dates: 2nd, 3rd, 22nd, 24th & 25th April; 1st, 2nd, 29th & 30th May; 4th, 5th, 12th, 19th & 26th June; 3rd, 10th, 17th, 24th & 31st July; 7th, 14th, 21st & 28th August; 18th September Trains usually run from every 35 minutes from around noon.
Note: Operating days may vary due to technical problems currently affecting the Gloucestershire & Warwickshire Railway.
Steam Working: Most operating days
Prices: Adults £2.00
Children £1.00 (Under-5s ride free)

Detailed Directions by Car:
Toddington is 11 miles north east of Cheltenham, 5 miles south of Broadway just off the B4632 (old A46). Exit the M5 at Junction 9 towards Stow-on-the-Wold for the B4632. The Railway is clearly visible from the B4632.

VALE OF RHEIDOL RAILWAY

Address: The Locomotive Shed, Park Avenue, Aberystwyth, Dyfed SY23 1PG
Telephone Nº: (01970) 625819
Year Formed: 1902
Location of Line: Aberystwyth to Devil's Bridge
Length of Line: 11¾ miles

Nº of Steam Locos: 3
Nº of Other Locos: 1
Approx Nº of Visitors P.A.: 38,000
Gauge: 1 foot 11¾ inches
Web site: www.rheidolrailway.co.uk

GENERAL INFORMATION

Nearest Mainline Station: Aberystwyth (adjacent)
Nearest Bus Station: Aberystwyth (adjacent)
Car Parking: Available on site
Coach Parking: Parking available 400 yards away
Souvenir Shop(s): Yes
Food & Drinks: Yes

SPECIAL INFORMATION

The journey between the stations take one hour in each direction. At Devil's Bridge there is a cafe, toilets, a picnic area and the famous Mynach Falls. The line climbs over 600 feet in 11¾ miles.

OPERATING INFORMATION

Opening Times: 2011 dates: Open almost every day from 2nd April to 29th October with some exceptions (mostly Sundays in April, May, June and September). Please phone the railway for further information.
Steam Working: All trains are steam-hauled. Trains run from 10.30am to 4.00pm on most days.
Prices: Adult Return £14.50
Senior Citizen Return £13.00
Child Return – First 2 children per adult pay £3.50 each. Further children pay £7.25 each

Detailed Directions by Car:
From the North take A487 into Aberystwyth. From the East take A470 and A44 to Aberystwyth. From the South take A487 or A485 to Aberystwyth. The Station is joined on to the Mainline Station in Alexandra Road.

Valley International Park Railway

Address: Valley International Park, Crossford, Carluke ML8 5NJ
Telephone Nº: (01555) 860150
Year Formed: 1992
Location of Line: Crossford, Lanarkshire
Length of Line: 1 mile
Nº of Steam Locos: None
Nº of Other Locos: 1
Approx Nº of Visitors P.A.: 100,000 (to the Park itself)
Gauge: 2 feet
Web site: www.valleyinternationalpark.com

GENERAL INFORMATION

Nearest Mainline Station: Carluke (2½ miles)
Nearest Bus Station: Lanark (5 miles)
Car Parking: Available on site
Coach Parking: Available
Souvenir Shop(s): Various retail outlets at the Park
Food & Drinks: Available

SPECIAL INFORMATION

The Valley International Park is adjacent to the River Clyde and has extensive child play facilities amongst other attractions.

OPERATING INFORMATION

Opening Times: Daily throughout the year except for Christmas Day and New Year's Day. Open from 10.00am to 5.00pm.
Steam Working: None
Prices: £2.00 per ride

Detailed Directions by Car:
From All Parts: Exit the M74 at Junction 7 and take the A72 towards Lanark. Turn left onto the B7056 at Crossford then take the first turning on the right after crossing the River Clyde for access to the Park.

Volks Electric Railway

Address: Arch 285, Madeira Drive, Brighton BN2 1EN
Telephone Nº: (01273) 292718
Year Formed: 1883
Location of Line: Brighton seafront
Length of Line: 1 mile
Nº of Steam Locos: None
Nº of Other Locos: 7
Approx Nº of Visitors P.A.: 250,000
Gauge: 2 feet 8½ inches
Web site: www.whitstablepier.com/volks

GENERAL INFORMATION

Nearest Mainline Station: Brighton (2 miles)
Nearest Bus Station: Brighton Pier (¼ mile)
Car Parking: Available on site
Coach Parking: Available
Souvenir Shop(s): Yes
Food & Drinks: Available

SPECIAL INFORMATION

Opened in 1883, Volk's Electric Railway is the world's oldest operating electric railway. The brainchild of inventor Magnus Volk, the railway runs for just over a mile along Brighton seafront between Aquarium (for Brighton Pier) and Black Rock (for the Marina).

OPERATING INFORMATION

Opening Times: 2011 dates: Daily from 22nd April to 30th September, usually from 10.00am to 5.00pm (later starts on Tuesdays and Fridays).
Steam Working: None
Prices: Adult Return £3.00 (Single £1.90)
Child Return £1.50 (Single £1.00)
Concessionary Return £1.90 (Single £1.20)
Family Return £6.70 (Single £4.00)

Detailed Directions by Car:
From All Parts: Take the A23/A27 to Brighton and the railway is located on the seafront adjacent to the Pier.

WATERWORKS RAILWAY

Address: Kew Bridge Steam Museum, Green Dragon Lane, Brentford TW8 0EN
Telephone Nº: (020) 8568-4757
Year Formed: 1986
Location of Line: Greater London
Length of Line: Under 1 mile
Nº of Steam Locos: 1
Nº of Other Locos: 1
Nº of Members: 750
Annual Membership Fee: £20.00 Adult
Approx Nº of Visitors P.A.: 20,000
Gauge: 2 feet
Web site: www.kbsm.org

GENERAL INFORMATION

Nearest Mainline Station: Kew Bridge (3 minute walk)
Nearest Bus Station: Bus stop across the road – Services 65, 267 and 237
Car Parking: Spaces for 43 cars available on site
Coach Parking: Available on site – book in advance
Souvenir Shop(s): Yes
Food & Drinks: Yes – at weekends only

SPECIAL INFORMATION

The Museum is a former Victorian Pumping Station with a collection of working Steam Pumping Engines. The Railway demonstrates typical water board use of Railways.

OPERATING INFORMATION

Opening Times: 11.00am to 4.00pm, from Tuesday to Sunday inclusive throughout the year (closed on Mondays except for Bank Holidays).
Steam Working: Sundays and Bank Holiday Mondays from April to October and also on other special event days.
Prices: Adult £9.50 (Annual ticket)
Child – Free if accompanied by Adults
Senior Citizen £8.50 (Annual ticket)

Detailed Directions by Car:
From All Parts: Exit the M4 at Junction 2 and follow the A4 to Chiswick Roundabout. Take the exit signposted for Kew Gardens & Brentford. Go straight on at the next two sets of traffic lights following A315 towards Brentford. After 2nd set of lights take the first right for the museum. The museum is next to the tall Victorian tower.

Wat Tyler Miniature Railway

Address: Pitsea Hall Lane, Pitsea, Basildon SS16 4UH
Telephone Nº: (01268) 275050
Year Formed: 1988
Location of Line: Basildon, Essex
Length of Line: 1 mile
Web site: www.wattylerminiaturerailway.com

Nº of Steam Locos: None
Nº of Other Locos: 2
Approx Nº of Visitors P.A.: 250,000 visitors to the Park – 20,000 rides
Gauge: 10¼ inches

GENERAL INFORMATION

Nearest Mainline Station: East Pitsea (½ mile)
Nearest Bus Station: Basildon (2 miles)
Car Parking: Available on site
Coach Parking: Available
Souvenir Shop(s): None
Food & Drinks: Available

SPECIAL INFORMATION

The railway is located in the Wat Tyler Country Park close to the site of a 19th Century explosives factory.

OPERATING INFORMATION

Opening Times: Weekends throughout the year and daily during School Holidays. Open 11.20am to 4.50pm.
Steam Working: None
Prices: Adult Return £2.50
Child Return £1.50

Detailed Directions by Car:
From All Parts: Exit the A13 at the Pitsea Flyover and follow signs for Wat Tyler Country Park which is approximately ½ mile on the right.

Wells Harbour Railway

Address: Wells Harbour Railway, Beach Road, Wells-next-the-Sea NR23 1DR
Telephone Nº: (07939) 149264
Year Formed: 1976
Location of Line: Wells-next-the-Sea
Length of Line: Approximately 1 mile

Nº of Steam Locos: None
Nº of Other Locos: 2
Approx Nº of Visitors P.A.: 50,000
Gauge: 10¼ inches
Web site: www.wellsharbourrailway.co.uk

GENERAL INFORMATION

Nearest Mainline Station: King's Lynn (21 miles)
Nearest Bus Station: Norwich (24 miles)
Car Parking: Public car parks near each station
Coach Parking: Available in town
Souvenir Shop(s): No
Food & Drinks: No

SPECIAL INFORMATION

Wells Harbour Railway was the first 10¼" narrow gauge railway to run a scheduled passenger service and is listed in the Guinness Book of Records!

OPERATING INFORMATION

Opening Times: Weekends from Easter until Spring Bank Holiday then daily through to the middle of September. Then weekends until the end of October. The first train departs at 10.30am.
Steam Working: None
Prices: Adult Single £1.30
Child Single £1.00

Detailed Directions by Car:
Wells-next-the-Sea is located on the North Norfolk cost between Hunstanton and Cromer. The railway is situated on Beach Road next to the harbour. Follow the signs for Pinewoods and Beach.

Wells & Walsingham Light Railway

Address: The Station, Wells-next-the-Sea NR23 1QB
Telephone Nº: (01328) 711630
Year Formed: 1982
Location of Line: Wells-next-the-Sea to Walsingham, Norfolk
Length of Line: 4 miles

Nº of Steam Locos: 2
Nº of Other Locos: 2
Nº of Members: 50
Annual Membership Fee: £11.00
Approx Nº of Visitors P.A.: 20,000
Gauge: 10¼ inches
Website: www.wellswalsinghamrailway.co.uk

GENERAL INFORMATION

Nearest Mainline Station: King's Lynn (21 miles)
Nearest Bus Station: Norwich (24 miles)
Car Parking: Free parking at site
Coach Parking: Free parking at site
Souvenir Shop(s): Yes
Food & Drinks: Yes

SPECIAL INFORMATION

The Railway is the longest 10¼ inch narrow-gauge steam railway in the world. The course of the railway is famous for wildlife and butterflies in season.

OPERATING INFORMATION

Opening Times: 2011 dates: Daily from 9th April until 29th October.
Steam Working: Trains run from 10.15am on operating days.
Prices: Adult Return £8.00
Child Return £6.50

Detailed Directions by Car:
Wells-next-the-Sea is situated on the North Norfolk Coast midway between Hunstanton and Cromer. The Main Station is situated on the main A149 Stiffkey Road. Follow the brown tourist signs for the Railway.

Welsh Highland Heritage Railway

Address: Tremadog Road, Porthmadog, Gwynedd LL49 9DY	**Nº of Steam Locos:** 3
Telephone Nº: (01766) 513402	**Nº of Other Locos:** 18
Year Formed: 1961	**Nº of Members:** 1,000
Location of Line: Opposite Porthmadog Mainline Station	**Annual Membership Fee:** £25.00 Adult
Length of Line: 1½ mile round trip	**Approx Nº of Visitors P.A.:** 25,000
	Gauge: 1 foot 11½ inches
	Web site: www.whr.co.uk

GENERAL INFORMATION

Nearest Mainline Station: Porthmadog (adjacent)
Nearest Bus Station: Services 1 & 3 stop 50 yards away
Car Parking: Free parking at site, plus a public Pay and Display car park within 100 yards
Coach Parking: Adjacent
Souvenir Shop(s): Yes – large range available
Food & Drinks: Yes – excellent home cooking at the Russell Team Room!

SPECIAL INFORMATION

The Welsh Highland Railway is a family-orientated attraction based around a Railway Heritage Centre and includes a guided, hands-on tour of the sheds. A ¾ mile extension to Traeth Mawr is now open.

OPERATING INFORMATION

Opening Times: 2011 dates: Daily from 26th March to 30th October inclusive (closed on some Mondays and Fridays during October). Trains run at 10.30am, 11.30am, 1.00pm, 2.00pm, 3.00pm and 4.00pm (the last train runs at 3.00pm during October and November).
Steam Working: 16th to 25th April; 1st & 2nd May; 28th May to 5th June; Weekends in June and July then daily from 23rd July to 4th September; Weekends in September; 22nd to 30th October.
Prices: Adult Day Rover £6.00
Child Day Rover £3.00 (Under-5s free)
Senior Citizen Day Rover £5.00
Family Day Rover £15.00
(2 adults + 2 children)

Detailed Directions by Car:
From Bangor/Caernarfon take the A487 to Porthmadog. From Pwllheli take the A497 to Porthmadog then turn left at the roundabout. From the Midlands take A487 to Portmadog. Once in Porthmadog, follow the brown tourist signs. The line is located right next to Porthmadog Mainline Station, opposite the Queens Hotel.

Welsh Highland Railway

Postal Address: Ffestiniog Railway, Harbour Station, Porthmadog LL49 9NF
Telephone Nº: (01766) 516000
Year Formed: 1997
Location: Caernarfon to Porthmadog
Length of Line: 25 miles
Nº of Steam Locos: 8 (5 working)
Nº of Other Locos: 3
Nº of Members: 2,300
Annual Membership Fee: £25.00
Approx Nº of Visitors P.A.: 80,000
Gauge: 1 foot 11½ inches
Web site: www.festrail.co.uk

GENERAL INFO

Nearest Mainline Station:
Porthmadog (½ mile) or Bangor (7 miles) (Bus service Nº 5 to Caernarfon)
Nearest Bus Station:
Porthmadog or Caernarfon
Car Parking:
Parking available at Caernarfon
Coach Parking:
At Victoria Docks (¼ mile from Caernarfon station) and in Porthmadog
Souvenir Shop(s): Yes
Food & Drinks:
Full buffet available on most trains

SPECIAL INFO

The Railway has been reconstructed between Caernarfon and Porthmadog along the track bed of the original Welsh Highland Railway. 2011 sees the completion of this spectacular route passing from coast to coast through the majestic scenery of the Snowdonia National Park.

OPERATING INFO

Opening Times: Regular services run from Easter to the end of October. There is also a limited service in the Winter. Train times vary depending on the date. Please contact the railway for further details.
Steam Working:
Most trains are steam-hauled.
Prices: Adult £32.00
(All-day Rover ticket)
One child travels free with each adult, additional children travel for half the fare. Concessionary prices are available for Senior Citizens and groups of 20 or more and cheaper fares are available for single rides and shorter journeys.

Detailed Directions by Car:
Take either the A487(T), the A4085 or the A4086 to Caernarfon then follow the brown tourist signs for the Railway which is situated in St. Helens Road next to the Castle.

WELSHPOOL & LLANFAIR LIGHT RAILWAY

Address: The Station, Llanfair Caereinion, Powys SY21 0SF
Telephone Nº: (01938) 810441
Year Formed: 1959
Location of Line: Welshpool to Llanfair Caereinion, Mid Wales
Length of Line: 8 miles
Nº of Steam Locos: 9
Nº of Other Locos: 5
Nº of Members: 1,900
Annual Membership Fee: £22.50
Approx Nº of Visitors P.A.: 26,000
Gauge: 2 feet 6 inches
Web site: www.wllr.org.uk

GENERAL INFORMATION

Nearest Mainline Station: Welshpool (1 mile)
Nearest Bus Station: Welshpool (1 mile)
Car Parking: Free parking at Welshpool and Llanfair Caereinion
Coach Parking: As above
Souvenir Shop(s): Yes – at both ends of line
Food & Drinks: Yes – at Llanfair only

SPECIAL INFORMATION

The railway has the steepest gradient of any British railway, reaching a summit of 603 feet.

OPERATING INFORMATION

Opening Times: 2011 dates: Daily from 16th to 25th April then weekends and Bank Holidays until 30th May. Daily from 31st May to 25th September but closed on most Fridays. Also open on weekends and daily during school holidays in October then for Santa Specials on 10th, 11th, 17th and 18th December. Generally open from 9.30am to 5.00pm.
Steam Working: All trains are steam-hauled
Prices: Adult £11.90
Senior Citizens £10.90
Children under the age of 3 travel free of charge.
The first child aged 3-15 per adult travels for £1.00.
All other children are charged half-price – £5.95

Detailed Directions by Car:
Both stations are situated alongside the A458 Shrewsbury to Dolgellau road and are clearly signposted

West Lancashire Light Railway

Address: Station Road, Hesketh Bank, Nr. Preston, Lancashire PR4 6SP
Telephone Nº: (01772) 815881
Year Formed: 1967
Location of Line: On former site of Alty's Brickworks, Hesketh Bank
Length of Line: ¼ mile

Nº of Steam Locos: 8
Nº of Other Locos: 24
Nº of Members: Approximately 110
Annual Membership Fee: £15.00 Adult; £20.00 Family
Approx Nº of Visitors P.A.: 14,500
Gauge: 2 feet
Web site: www.westlancs.org

GENERAL INFORMATION

Nearest Mainline Station: Rufford (4 miles)
Nearest Bus Station: Preston (7 miles)
Car Parking: Space for 50 cars at site
Coach Parking: Space for 3 coaches at site
Souvenir Shop(s): Yes
Food & Drinks: Only soft drinks & snacks

SPECIAL INFORMATION

The Railway is run by volunteers and there is a large collection of Industrial Narrow Gauge equipment.

OPERATING INFORMATION

Opening Times: 2011 dates: Sundays and Bank Holidays from 3rd April to 30th October and also for Santa Specials from 11th, 17th, 18th and 24th December. Trains run from 11.30am to 5.00pm.
Steam Working: Trains operate on Sundays and Bank Holidays from April until the end of October.
Prices: Adult £4.00 Child £3.00
Family Tickets £6.00
Senior Citizens £3.50
Note: Different fares apply for Gala Days and Santa Specials.

Detailed Directions by Car:
Travel by the A59 from Liverpool or Preston or by the A565 from Southport to the junction of the two roads at Tarleton. From here follow signs to Hesketh Bank. The Railway is signposted.

WINDMILL ANIMAL FARM RAILWAY

Address: Windmill Animal Farm,
Red Cat Lane, Burscough L40 1UQ
Telephone Nº: (07971) 221343
Year Formed: 1997
Location of Line: Burscough, Lancashire
Length of Line: 1 mile

Nº of Steam Locos: 5
Nº of Other Locos: 6
Nº of Members: 7
Annual Membership Fee: None
Approx Nº of Visitors P.A.: 40,000
Gauge: 15 inches
Web: www.windmillanimalfarm.co.uk

GENERAL INFORMATION

Nearest Mainline Station: Burscough (2½ miles)
Nearest Bus Station: Southport (8½ miles)
Car Parking: Available at the Farm
Coach Parking: Available at the Farm
Souvenir Shop(s): Yes
Food & Drinks: Available

SPECIAL INFORMATION

In addition to the railway, the site includes a play area and a large number of farm animals with a petting area where children can feed the animals.

OPERATING INFORMATION

Opening Times: 2011 dates: Open Daily from 2nd April until the end of September and during weekends and school holidays at all other times. 11.00am to 5.00pm.
Steam Working: Every weekend
Prices: Adult Admission £6.00 (Farm entrance)
Child Admission £5.00 (Farm entrance)
Family Admission £18.00 (Farm entrance)
Train Rides: Adult £1.50
Child £1.00

Detailed Directions by Car:
From All Parts: Exit the M6 at Junction 27 and take the A5209 following signs for Southport. On entering Burscough follow signs for Burscough Bridge and Martin Lane. Turn left into Red Cat Lane just by Burscough Bridge train station and follow the road along for Windmill Animal Farm and the Railway.

Woodhorn Narrow Gauge Railway

Address: Woodhorn Northumberland Museum, Queen Elizabeth II Country Park, Ashington NE63 9YF
Telephone Nº: (01670) 528080
Year Formed: 1995
Location of Line: Northumberland
Length of Line: 1,000 yards

Nº of Steam Locos: None
Nº of Other Locos: 2
Approx Nº of Visitors P.A.: 100,000 (to the museum)
Gauge: 2 feet
Web site: www.experiencewoodhorn.com

GENERAL INFORMATION

Nearest Mainline Station: Morpeth (8 miles)
Nearest Bus Station: Ashington (1 mile)
Car Parking: Available on site
Coach Parking: Available
Souvenir Shop(s): Yes
Food & Drinks: Available

SPECIAL INFORMATION

The railway runs through the grounds of the Woodhorn Northumberland Museum and is operated by volunteers.

OPERATING INFORMATION

Opening Times: Wednesdays and weekends throughout the year and daily during School Holidays, weather permitting. Open from 10.00am to 5.00pm (4.00pm during the Winter months). Closed during all Bank Holidays.
Steam Working: None
Prices: Adults £2.00
Children £1.00

Detailed Directions by Car:
From All Parts: Take the A1 to the A19 at Cramlington then the A189 towards Ashington and follow the brown tourist signs for Woodhorn. (Beware of SatNav directions which may leave you on the wrong side of the local goods railway line!)

Woodland Railway

Address: Brokerswood Country Park, Westbury BA13 4EH
Telephone Nº: (01373) 822238
Year Formed: –
Location of Line: West Wiltshire
Length of Line: Two-thirds of a mile
Nº of Steam Locos: None
Nº of Other Locos: 1
Approx Nº of Visitors P.A.: 60,000
Gauge: 10¼ inches
Web site: www.brokerswoodcountrypark.co.uk

GENERAL INFORMATION

Nearest Mainline Station: Westbury (2 miles)
Nearest Bus Station: Bath (12 miles)
Car Parking: Available on site
Coach Parking: Available
Souvenir Shop(s): Yes
Food & Drinks: Available

SPECIAL INFORMATION

The railway runs through the award-winning Brokerswood Country Park, a precious 80 acre fragment of the ancient forest of Selwood.

OPERATING INFORMATION

Opening Times: Weekends and daily during the School Holidays from Easter until the end of October. Open from 10.00am to 5.00pm.
Steam Working: None
Prices: Adult Return £1.00
Child Return £1.00

Detailed Directions by Car:
From All Parts: Exit the M4 at Junction 18 and take the A46 to Bath then the A36 to Beckington services. Turn left onto the A361 towards Southwick then follow the brown tourist signs to Brokerswood Country Park.